Lecture Notes in Computer Scie

Commenced Publication in 1973
Founding and Former Series Editors:
Gerhard Goos, Juris Hartmanis, and Jan van Leeuwen

Jobst Löffler   Markus Klann (Eds.)

Mobile Response

Second International Workshop
on Mobile Information Technology
for Emergency Response, MobileResponse 2008
Bonn, Germany, May 29-30, 2008
Revised Selected Papers

 Springer

Volume Editors

Jobst Löffler
Fraunhofer IAIS
Schloss Birlinghoven
53754 Sankt Augustin
Germany
E-mail: jobst.loeffler@iais.fraunhofer.de

Markus Klann
Fraunhofer FIT
Schloss Birlinghoven
53754 Sankt Augustin
Germany
E-mail: markus.klann@fit.fraunhofer.de

Library of Congress Control Number: 2009921606

CR Subject Classification (1998): H.5.2, H.5.3, H.2.8, H.3-5, C.2, J.1

LNCS Sublibrary: SL 5 – Computer Communication Networks
and Telecommunications

ISSN   0302-9743
ISBN-10   3-642-00439-3 Springer Berlin Heidelberg New York
ISBN-13   978-3-642-00439-1 Springer Berlin Heidelberg New York

springer.com

© Springer-Verlag Berlin Heidelberg 2009
Printed in Germany

Typesetting: Camera-ready by author, data conversion by Scientific Publishing Services, Chennai, India
Printed on acid-free paper   SPIN: 12619740   06/3180   5 4 3 2 1 0

Preface

Mobile Response 2008, the Second International Workshop on Mobile Information Technology for Emergency Response, aimed at a focussed exchange on how mobile information technology can be effectively used to the benefit of emergency response. The gap between the great potential benefit that usable mobile IT could yield in the domain of emergency response and the specific design challenges for such technologies in this particularly unforgiving domain was the foundation of our decision to create a venue for researchers and practitioners from different disciplines. During this year's workshop the latest approaches and technical solutions in the area of mobile information technology for emergency response planning and execution were presented and demonstrated.

We invited participation from research, industry and public rescue organizations to enable an in-depth discussion of the opportunities and drawbacks of new digital technologies for emergency response. The call for papers for the second Mobile Response workshop attracted over 25 submissions from 11 different countries, including international submissions from the USA, Brazil and Japan. An international Program Committee with experts on mobile information technology, emergency response and emergency response equipment selected 12 submissions for presentation during the workshop. The program was completed by two outstanding keynote presentations and one invited presentation on prevailing topics of high interest to the scientific and practitioner communities.

Mobile Response 2008 was held during May 29–30 on the premises of the Bonn-Aachen International Center for Information Technology in Bonn, Germany. The presentations offered not only an interesting overview of how different disciplines address the design of mobile IT, but also provided insight into the perspectives from different countries as well as the different perspectives of scientists, industrial representatives and practitioners. The interesting discussions during the workshop raised important questions from which the following were identified as most pressing:

1. How can the apparent gap between practitioners' needs and promising research efforts be bridged with a strong involvement of industry?

2. Can mobile ICT help reduce complexity in disaster management and emergency response work? Or does it actually introduce new complexity to the situation.

3. How can we bring research prototypes to product level and introduce them to the daily work of practitioners? How can a successful knowledge transfer be established?

We expect these issues to be the focus of the community's activies in the next few years.

We would like to thank the members of the Program Committee who were very helpful in attracting attention to the event and reviewing the submissions. We would like to thank everybody who was involved in the preparation of the event, particularly our colleagues from Fraunhofer IAIS and Fraunhofer FIT. Most importantly we would like to thank everybody who submitted to Mobile Response 2008, all the presenters and all the participants who contributed to an intriguing exchange during the event. Special thanks go to our keynote presenters Chris Johnson (Glasgow University) and Bartel Van de Walle (Tilburg University) who gave most interesting talks and participated in the lively discussions during the two-day event with huge enthusiasm. After having organized two very successful workshops in 2007 and 2008, we plan to continue with Mobile Response in 2009 and would like to invite everybody interested to check www.mobile-response.org for announcements on this event.

July 2008   Jobst Löffler
                                                                                 Markus Klann

Organization

Mobile Response 2008 was organized by the Fraunhofer Institute for Intelligent Analysis and Information Systems IAIS and the Fraunhofer Institute for Applied Information Technology FIT. The symposium took place during May 29–30, 2008, on the premises of the Bonn-Aachen International Center for Information Technology B-IT in Bonn, Germany.

Organizing Committee

Workshop Co-chair	Jobst Löffler (Fraunhofer IAIS, Germany)
Workshop Co-chair	Markus Klann (Fraunhofer FIT, Germany)

Referees

C. Baber	J. Köhler	G. Rigoll
S. Boll	M. Larson	L.M.A. Santos
M. Borges	M. Lawo	A. Schmidt
L. Chittaro	P. Lukowicz	B. Van de Walle
O. Herzog	A. Meissner	S. Wrobel
R. Ianella	K. Nieuwenhuis	V. Wulf
M. Jarke	B. Pavard	
C. Johnson	I. Pitas	
R. Koch	E. Raybourn	

Table of Contents

Communication and Security Concepts

Complexity, Structured Chaos and the Importance of Information Management for Mobile Computing in the UK Floods of 2007

Christopher W. Johnson

Department of Computing Science, University of Glasgow,
Glasgow, Scotland, G12 8RZ, UK
johnson@dcs.gla.ac.uk

Abstract. Many research teams have developed mobile computing architectures to support the emergency and rescue services in a range of civil contingencies. These proposals are based on innovative technologies and show considerable creativity in the design of their user interfaces. In contrast, this paper presents lessons learned from the 2007 UK floods. Mobile telecommunications failed in many different ways and from many different causes, including physical damage to handsets, as well as the loss of base stations and UPSs. The insights gained from the floods are being used to inform the design of next generation mobile digital communications systems for UK responders. However, the technical problems are arguably less important than the insights that were obtained about 'systemic' failures in the interfaces between local government, emergency services and the variety of agencies that must cooperate in major civil contingencies. Problems in information management led to inconsistencies and incompatibilities. In consequence, the output from one application could not easily be used as input to systems operated by other agencies. These issues must be addressed before we are overwhelmed by the increased bandwidth afforded by new mobile devices and novel sensing technologies. It is concluded that unless we understand the chaos, complexity and the contextual issues that characterise previous emergency situations then there is little prospect that we will be able to design effective mobile technologies for future incidents.

Keywords: accident analysis; national critical infrastructures; mobile devices.

1 Introduction

There have been a number of innovative proposals for the application of mobile computing technologies to support the emergency services. These include systems that focus on small teams of co-workers [1] as well as those that support large distributed organizations [12]. They include applications that provide structured interfaces to mobile systems for emergency workers [13] as well as less formal networking applications that support diverse group of end-users [10]. Other research teams have extended conventional evaluation techniques from desktop systems to support the validation of human-computer interaction with mobile devices by teams of emergency

J. Löffler and M. Klann (Eds.): Mobile Response, LNCS 5424, pp. 1–11, 2009.

workers [4]. Other groups have extended ideas from pervasive and ubiquitous computing [2]; including the development of 'wearable' devices to support interaction with computational infrastructures during emergency situations [6].

1.1   Strengths of Mobile Systems in Civil Contingencies

Most of these initiatives are based on the assumption that mobile computational systems provide significant value beyond traditional voice communication applications [9]. Mobile systems can be used by emergency personnel 'on site' during a contingency to navigate across multiple information sources held by different government and commercial agencies. This flexibility is critical when data cannot easily be formatted or structured in a way that will support the detailed requirements of every potential emergency. PDAs and similar devices provide a common interface to a vast array of information resources, including but not limited to census data, medical records, hazard information (e.g., flood predictions, location of hazardous substances etc), and weather details. Mobile computer systems can be integrated with digital telecommunications infrastructures to provide real-time updates as information becomes available. They can reduce the need to manually update paper-maps with the changing locations of emergency crews and with information about potential casualties. Images of an emergency can be communicated back from mobile devices on the scene of a civil contingency to help improve the situation awareness of co-workers and of coordinators in remote locations.

1.2   Concerns about Mobile Systems in Civil Contingencies

Changes to the technological infrastructure of complex systems cannot be 'risk free' [5]. The provision of new services creates new hazards, for example when users have to cope with the failure of services normally provided using mobile technology. Further problems arise when mobile systems are poorly integrated into existing working practices. The UK Independent Police Complaints Commission (IPCC) recently described how the driver of a marked police car was responding to the activation of his vehicle's automatic number plate recognition system, when a pedestrian was hit and killed [3]. Similarly, the US National Oceanic & Atmospheric Administration (NOAA) released a warning in 2002 about some of the systemic effects of GPS on navigation behavior. These warnings were addressed to all users of mobile devices including emergency personnel. NOAA went on to point out that the increasing accuracy of GPS exposes underlying problems in the accuracy of charts. Many maps were developed using less accurate fixes than those provided using GPS technology. It was argued that prudent users should employ "the utmost caution, no matter what navigational method is used" [8].

1.3   Overview of the Paper

The following pages collect together a number of lessons that were learned about the application of mobile technologies from the 2007 UK floods. These included insights about the vulnerability of the mobile telecommunications infrastructures that support many of the technical innovations proposed in previous studies. The floods also revealed underlying problems in information management that frustrated attempts to coordinate data exchange between different agencies.

Other insights included the importance of helping members of the public to access information from a wide range of sources, ranging from local government to the police, from insurance companies to utility companies. In many cases, individuals and families had a range of existing devices that could have provided access to critical information even though there were problems with the telecommunications infrastructure. Many failed to find the details that they needed to protect themselves and their family because the information was not structured in a way that could easily be downloaded onto available devices. Critical data was often scattered over different web sites or between on-line resources and through telephone 'hot lines'. It is concluded that we must develop a more coordinated approach to information management in order to design mobile technologies that can be used by emergency personnel and the general public in future contingencies.

2   The Scale of the Floods and the Need for Mobile Resources

Many areas of the United Kingdom experienced their heaviest rainfall since records began between May and July 2007. Precipitation exacerbated high levels of ground water. This combination overwhelmed drains and other forms of flood defence. The UK Meteorological Office recorded 414.1mm of rain across England and Wales; this is over double the mean level of rainfall expected during this period. The most severe floods occurred across Northern Ireland on 12th June; East Yorkshire and areas of the Midlands on 15th June; Yorkshire, Gloucestershire and Worcestershire on 25th June; and Oxfordshire, Berkshire and South Wales on 20th July. The independent report into the subsequent floods, chaired by Sir Michael Pitt [11], argued that these events created "a new level of challenge" for emergency personnel; triggering "a series of emergencies which stretched local resources to the limit" and which provided UK civil contingency planners with a "wake-up call".

2.1   Impact on the Transportation and Supply Infrastructures

The consequences of the floods are difficult to exaggerate. They continue to affect the lives of many families that were caught up in them. This natural civil contingency has been linked to 13 deaths as well as damage to over 40,000 homes and 10,000 businesses. In some places, the floodwaters rose over a number of hours. In other areas, emergency service personnel and members of the public were left stranded as flood defences failed and roads were closed. Five hundred people were left on the platforms and concourse areas of Gloucester railway station on the night of the 20th July as areas of the UK national rail network were disabled. At the same time, approximately 10,000 motorists were stranded by the closure of Junctions 10 to 12 on the M5 motorway. The interruptions to transportation infrastructure had knock-on effects for the logistics of recovery operations as food, oil and personnel had to be re-routed to take account of successive closures across the transportation networks.

2.2 Impact on the Water Infrastructures

The coordination of civil contingencies in the UK is divided between three levels. Bronze describes the operational management of an incident usually on-site. Silver level refers to tactical management; operating remotely providing the resources to implement pre-determined contingency plans. Gold command defines the overall strategy for resolving an incident and coordinates recovery actions. The Pitt interim report describes how Gloucestershire Gold Command group convened around 18:00 on Friday, 20th July 2007 [11]. The Environment Agency reported that they did not expect any significant river flooding. The same evening, the Meteorological Office warned that heavy rain was expected to continue overnight. The Gold Command held a teleconference to review the situation around 10.30 on Saturday 21st July. The Environment Agency again said that it expected little or no serious flooding. In consequence, a further meeting was held at 18:00 before the Gold command group disbanded for the evening. During the early hours of the 22nd, the Mythe water treatment works was shut down by rising flood water and serious flooding occurred in urban areas. The Gold command group was hastily reconvened. Water supplies in the area were not declared fit again until the 7th August. A collection of agencies responded to this and similar problems across the flooded areas, including the Army and the Red Cross. However, it is estimated that in several areas it was only possible to provide 10 litres per person per day well short of the 15-20 litres recommended by the World Health Organisation [11]. Members of the public were engaged in increasingly frantic searches for drinking water.

2.3 Impact on the Power Infrastructures

Rising levels of ground water also began to affect the integrity of dams, for example at Ulley reservoir, near Rotherham. This posed considerable risks both for the local population and for a host of other infrastructure assets. Such effects were only part of wider disruption across the electricity distribution networks. On 23rd July, the loss of the Castle Meads sub-station affected approximately 42,000 people in Gloucester. In Yorkshire, 4 major sub-stations and 55 secondary sub-stations were flooded causing more than 130,000 people to lose their supply. Similarly, the Walham switch station provided an interface to the UK high-voltage network for almost 500,000 people across Wales and Gloucestershire. As the waters from the River Severn rose, it became clear that this major infrastructure component was at significant risk. Members of the fire and rescue service, the Armed Forces, the Environment Agency and the National Grid assembled defences that eventually prevented the loss of the station. A previous risk assessment had assessed the risk of flooding for this site to be 1 in 1,000 per annum, an estimate that has been raised in 2005 to between 1 in 75 and 1 in 200 [11].

2.4 Impact on the Telecommunications Infrastructures

Telecommunications companies suffered considerable losses as floodwater began to infiltrate critical equipment. Further damage was caused by soil erosion and consequence cable breakages. Knock-on effects propagated from the loss of mains supplies as mobile base stations were forced rely on Uninterruptible Power Supplies (UPS). Backup generators began to run short of fuel and battery based systems were lost after a few hours. Internet routers were affected in a similar manner. The consequences were compounded by the numbers of users competed for remaining bandwidth in order to transfer critical digital information and to remain in contact with co-workers or family members. The effects of these interruptions were, however, mitigated by local Internet Service Providers who made ad hoc arrangements using borrowed generators and rerouting facilities to offer limited access for some users in the affected communities.

3 Mobile Response and the Emergency Services' Perspective

In retrospect, many telecommunications companies were surprised by the resilience of networks that continued to function even in areas of considerable flooding. The increasing use of optical fibre rather than copper cabling partly helps to explain why some communities were able to access digital infrastructures. The floods also reinforced the need to bring telecommunications and energy infrastructure managers into Gold command at an earlier stage in order to help coordinate the defence of both conventional and mobile infrastructures.

3.1 Demonstrating the Potential of Mobile Digital Technologies

Other lessons focussed more narrowly on the deployment of mobile telecommunications infrastructures. Gloucestershire Fire and Rescue Service's Incident Command Unit (ICU) used satellite communications to enable Internet access during July 2007. The ICU initially provided a central point of reference for the public but had to be redeployed as priorities changed. It was moved to coordinate the defence of the Castel Meads station, mentioned above. This redeployment is instructive because it shows how mobile resources can be moved to meet the changing priorities of civil contingencies. The redeployment of the Gloucestershire ICU also illustrates the benefits of mobile systems that can be used to satisfy multiple roles – both in supporting the general public and also in coordinating the response of emergency personnel.

The floods also illustrated the benefits of a new generation of digital telecommunications systems, such as Airwave. Many of these applications provide multiple levels of redundancy so that voice communication can be maintained even when elements of the underlying infrastructure have failed. Networks of base stations provided a technical backbone that enabled police to communicate with other emergency services over a common network. However, the floods reiterated the limitations of voice communications systems during civil contingencies. There were many situations in which emergency responders reported the need to transfer images or other documents that might have avoided lengthy discussions over devices with finite battery power. In particular, problems arose when emergency services tried to request support from neighbouring organisations. Direct voice messages asking for assistance had to be forwarded up the chain of command until they were relayed to officers and management staff with sufficient authority to approve the request. This led to frustration and delays especially when requests were refused. This occurred, for example, when neighbouring Fire and Rescue Authorities' were themselves struggling to secure necessary resources ranging from sandbags to drinking water or high volume pumping equipment.

At the time of the floods, several projects were underway to automate requests for support using digital data exchange. The UK FiReControl project is intended to provide firefighters with data terminals on their vehicles that can present a wide of information, including mapping and incident data, through a standard interface [7]. Similarly, the Firelink project will deliver a digital radio network for the Fire and Rescue Services (FRS) in England, Scotland and Wales that can be interoperated with all Fire and Rescue Authorities and with other emergency services. However, these facilities were not widely available across all of the FRS' involved in the immediate response to the 2007 floods. Even those authorities that had digital communications did not have sufficient devices for their needs.

The UK Chief Fire and Rescue Adviser's review also argued that the floods helped to highlight the differences in terms of the technology that was currently available in Fire and Rescue Services control rooms [7]. Mobile data capability is available 'at some level' in just over half of the 46 Fire and Rescue Authorities. Only two use it for the 'mobile scenarios' envisaged by the FiReControl project. Nine more have the capacity to support Mobile Data Terminals but there are strong differences in the ways that the systems will be used. Organizational and political barriers have created a situation in which there is no national capability to mobilize the nearest appropriate resource regardless of ownership.

3.2 Organizational Barriers to the Effective Use of Mobile Telecommunications

The floods of 2007 highlighted the non-technical problems that complicate the deployment and operation of mobile computer systems. Subsequent enquiries have considered how projects, such as FiReControl, could enable users to request assistance from neighbouring agencies [7]. In particular, attention has focused on the protocols that might enable a member of the Fire and Rescue Service at the scene of an incident to ask for additional resources from a Remote Control Centre (RCC). This centre could be tens or hundreds of miles from the scene of any contingency. One proposal being considered by the FiReControl project enables one centre to automatically detect when another, local RCC could no longer cope with the demands being placed on it. The Remote Control Centre might then mobilise resources that would normally be under the control of the local centre. Such scenarios are not normally the focus of mobile systems research. Most previous work focuses on technical infrastructures or user interface characteristics. However, these proposals create significant concerns for local centres who must maintain sufficient situation awareness to recognise when some of 'their' resources have been redeployed by the remote intervention of another RCC.

In contrast, Gloucestershire Fire and Rescue Authority reported that having Gold Command bases close to the local mobilising centre had 'significant operational benefits'. They were also 'concerned about how this would work once the Remote Control Centre was in place' [7]. The meta-level point here is that unless the research and development community pay close attention to the insights from previous contingencies then there is a danger that we will develop systems which do not address the concerns of operational staff with first-hand experience in trying to manage the 'structured chaos' and the complexity of real-world events.

In the UK, there is a distinction between category 1 and category 2 responders. The former include the Police, Fire and Rescue Services, Emergency Medical Services, the Coastguard, Local Authorities, Primary Care Trusts, Acute Trusts, Foundation Trusts etc. Category 2 responders include Electricity Distributors and Transmitters, Gas Distributors, Water and Sewerage companies, Telephone service providers (fixed and mobile). They also include the transport sector, including Network Rail, Train Operating Companies (passenger and freight), Underground companies, the Highways Agency, Airport operators etc. The floods illustrated considerable problems in coordinating the activities of category 1 and 2 responders. Many category 2 agencies were unaware of the procedures and protocols used by Gold Command and hence found it difficult to contribute in the manner that had been anticipated. Further problems arose from the confusion over the lead agency for dealing with floods. At the time of writing this paper, the precise division of responsibilities between Fire and Rescue Services, the Maritime and Coastguard Agency, the RNLI, river police etc is unclear. This lack of clarity complicates future inter-agency cooperation, which in turn, has the potential to undermine the benefits of technical innovation through the deployment of mobile systems.

The ability to communicate during contingency is facilitated by the provision of mobile technologies. However, many category 2 groups are not covered by the mobile infrastructures identified in previous sections of this paper. Many of them have no means of accessing the digital communications infrastructures available to the category 1 responders. This creates significant barriers to the 'seamless' transmission of digital information that many people have anticipated. The use of the name 'Firelink' to describe the digital radio network for the Fire and Rescue Services (FRS) illustrates some of the design assumptions behind these infrastructures. Applications that have been developed primarily to support the response to fires cannot always be redeployed for use in flood rescues from inflatable dinghies. Similarly, there can be significant inter-operability issues between this new generation of digital communications infrastructure and the wider stakeholders in any response to civil contingencies.

3.3 Information Management Barriers to the Use of Mobile Digital Telecomms

The organisational issues that complicated the response to the 2007 floods were exacerbated by a number of concerns that had not been anticipated during contingency planning. Many of these issues stemmed from legal 'myths' about civil liberties. This aspect is also often overlooked by the proponents of mobile systems but was a significant issue for many of the agencies involved in the flood response. Members of the Fire and Rescue Services were tasked to offer assistance to the elderly and to other 'at risk' groups in the communities affected by the rising waters. However, in order to find the addresses of people who might need help, they were forced to consult local healthcare organisations, self-help groups etc. Many of these agencies were unwilling to release personal details of their clients even under during severe flooding. Individuals felt that by disclosing this data they would be liable under European human rights legislation and the UK Data Protection Act. Cabinet Office guidance makes it clear that public safety overrides many of these concerns during civil contingencies. However, this message did not reach many of the emergency workers in the field.

The 'myths' surrounding the UK Data Protection Act form part of a wider pattern of confusion, contradiction and inconsistency that characterised many aspects of the information interchange that took place between local and national agencies during the floods. It is to be hoped that the proposed mobile computational systems will address many of these problems. However, there is a considerable risk that Gold and Silver commands will be overwhelmed by the data from the proposed new generation of handheld data terminals. Conversely, there is a risk that few category 1 responders will have time to use many of the facilities offered by these mobile systems.

The UK Cabinet Office had an almost continual need for information from local agencies to help form the 'big picture' during the floods of 2007. Some Gold and Silver commands were swamped by requests for information. At the same time, many were focused on acting at a local level. They often did not prioritise these requests from national agencies if they were not perceived to directly help the people caught up in local flooding. The extent of the confusion can be illustrated by the difficulty that central government faced in determining how many people had been affected by the June floods. Initial reports from the Environment Agency suggested that between 3,000 and 4,000 properties were affected [11]. Several days later, Government Offices and local authorities reported that 30,000 houses were flooded. The discrepancy arose because the Environment Agency only counted properties affected by river flooding. It excluded surface water flooding of urban properties that was the most significant source of damage during June 2007. These differences create enormous problems that cannot easily be addressed through the introduction of mobile computing devices unless they are accompanied by a root and branch reform of the information management systems across national and local government.

Not only did central government receive a confused picture from local agencies, those agencies themselves had a 'poor understanding of the location of critical sites; the mapping of their vulnerability to flooding; the consequences of their loss; and dependencies on other critical infrastructure' [11]. There was a need for first responders to have up-to-date flood risk information to coordinate their efforts in helping the public. This data was also important to ensure that emergency personnel did not expose themselves or their vehicles to additional hazards. Such risk assessments create a requirement to integrate meteorological forecasting, with environmental and urban models that consider critical infrastructures. Responders must also be able to access warnings issued by many other agencies, for example to ensure that they are aware of changes in the level of a water course, or to determine whether or not a power cable is live, or to determine the degree of risk posed by structural damage to a dam. None of these issues directly related to the development of mobile computational infrastructures. Those agencies that deployed the new generation digital systems reported considerable satisfaction, although there were some caveats about the need for more devices and more robust user interfaces [7]. The real problems stem from the institutional and organisational barriers to information interchange. For example, different government agencies used different mapping systems. This made it difficult to share data – for instance about flood levels and the location of 'at risk' members of the public or the location of Fire and Rescue Personnel and the state of local critical infrastructures. In the aftermath of the floods, it was proposed that the 'use of flood related data on Mobile Data Terminals as part of the FiReControl/Firelink projects should be considered' [7]. Only with the benefit of hindsight can we argue that such requirements should have been central to the initial design of any future mobile system for national civil contingencies.

4 Mobile Response and the General Public's Perspective

Previous paragraphs have focused on the mobile infrastructures from the perspective of emergency workers. We have ignored the information requirements of the families and individuals that were caught up in the floods. The Pitt review describes how one family saw water pour through the door of their home [11]. They asked the council for sandbags, which arrived one week later and after their property had sustained significant damage. When he called the Fire and Rescue Service, the father was put through to a different county. We have already described how the FireControl and similar projects are planning to support this load balancing do that one authority can aid another. In this case, however, the neighboring Fire and Rescue Service was not able to provide help. The home owner was concerned that the water in his house was contaminated and so decided to move. The council told him to go to a local leisure center – he drove his family at some risk through the flood waters only to find that had been given the wrong information. It was not being used as a rest center.

It is important to look at the wider 'systems level' issues that prevented the dissemination of information to the public. The loss of mains power in many areas disrupted the use of mains radios, televisions, computers and fixed line telephones. Problems with routers and with mobile base stations gradually began to affect other forms of portable telecommunication. However, information was still conveyed using door-to-door calls to vulnerable people; sirens, loudhailers, PA announcements [7, 11]. Previous sections have also stressed that many aspects of the infrastructure were surprisingly resilient and so many members of the public received information using electronic messages on motorways; automated telephone messages, fax, email, SMS texts; television and radio.

Ad hoc combinations of the existing communications channels were used to convey critical information to the public in the same way that emergency personnel found ways to 'work around' problems in their mobile and fixed telecommunications infrastructure. A key lesson learned from the 2007 floods for informing both the public and emergency responders was that the technology was arguably less important than the message itself. Just as the Fire and Rescue Services found difficulty in interpreting the risk assessments and warnings from other agencies, so also the general public had great problems in using the information that was eventually passed to them. One businessman noted that "The websites don't actually say Tesco's car park is going to flood – it's this tributary and that confluence – for people who don't have a geographical knowledge of rivers, it's almost impossible to weigh what's at threat and what's not" [11].

The lack of integrated information management systems affected the public as much as they did category 1 and category 2 responders. Individuals were forced to search through dozens of web sites to find information about insurance claims, about whether or not they could drink the water in their mains supply, about the disconnection or restoration of electricity; about the risk of further flooding. These sites were usually overloaded with enquiries and response times were very poor. This led to further frustration. "The thing that I found most difficult, as a company trying to keep 34 people going, and in the end we relied on Severn Sound (a local radio station) and the website, was to find out what was the truth about water. Can you drink it? Can you use it in the dishwasher? Can you boil it? They didn't know and they said first it wasn't drinkable" [11]. The provision of advanced mobile computational infrastructures is only one small part of the wider set of measures that are required to ensure that the public are never again left in such uncertainty over basic information requirements in the aftermath of civil contingencies.

5 Conclusions and Further Work

This paper has presented a number of lessons learned from the 2007 UK floods. Mobile telecommunications failed in many different ways. There were problems with using handsets that were designed to be operated in vehicles or on foot as emergency personnel struggled to reach families and individuals in dinghies or by wading through water. Other failures were caused by battery failures as the floods persisted over several days. Some agencies had access to newer forms of digital communication, including Air-Wave. However, they did not have enough devices to support the range of operations they were being expected to perform. These issues were compounded by failures in less resilient communications infrastructures, caused by the loss of base stations and UPSs. Such problems particularly affected coordination between category 1 responders and the category 2 groups, which are often overlooked during the deployment of more resilient mobile communications systems.

These technical issues are arguably less important than the insights that were obtained about 'systemic' failures in the interfaces between local government, emergency services and the variety of agencies that must cooperate in major civil contingencies. In particular, problems in information management led to inconsistencies and incompatibilities both at the level of individual data items, including assessments of the number of properties affected, and at the systems level, for instance between the data format used by Geographical Information Systems. In consequence, the output from one application could not easily be used as input to systems operated by other groups of responders. These issues must be addressed before we are overwhelmed by the increased bandwidth afforded by new mobile computing devices and novel sensing technologies. Unless we understand the chaos, complexity and the contextual issues that characterise previous emergency situations then there is little prospect that we will be able to design effective mobile technologies for future contingencies.

Acknowledgments. Thanks are due to the members of the Pitt review team whose work has motivated and informed the argument in this paper.

References

1. Auriol, E.: AMIRA: Advanced Multi-modal Intelligence for Remote Assistance. In: Löffler, J., Klann, M. (eds.) Mobile Response 2007. LNCS, vol. 4458, pp. 51–60. Springer, Heidelberg (2007)
2. Baber, C., Cross, J., Smith, P., Robinson, D.: Supporting Implicit Coordination Between Distributed Teams in Disaster Management. In: Löffler, J., Klann, M. (eds.) Mobile Response 2007. LNCS, vol. 4458, pp. 39–50. Springer, Heidelberg (2007)
3. BBC New, Arrests follow police car death (May 21, 2008) (last accessed June 23, 2008), http://news.bbc.co.uk/1/hi/england/tyne/7410441.stm

4. Chittaro, L., Zuliani, F., Carchietti, E.: Mobile Devices in Emergency Medical Services: User Evaluation of a PDA-based Interface for Ambulance Run Reporting. In: Löffler, J., Klann, M. (eds.) Mobile Response 2007. LNCS, vol. 4458, pp. 20–29. Springer, Heidelberg (2007)
5. Johnson, C.W.: A Handbook of Accident and Incident Reporting, University of Glasgow Press, Glasgow (2003) (last accessed June 24, 2008), http://www.dcs.gla.ac.uk/~johnson/book
6. Klann, M.: Playing with Fire: User-Centered Design of Wearable Computing for Emergency Response. In: Löffler, J., Klann, M. (eds.) Mobile Response 2007. LNCS, vol. 4458, pp. 116–125. Springer, Heidelberg (2007)
7. Knight, S.K.: Facing the Challenge: The Chief Fire and Rescue Adviser's review of the operational response by the Fire and Rescue Service to the widespread flooding in England during 2007, Department for Communities and Local Government, London, UK (March 2008)
8. National Imagery and Mapping Agency, Using Nautical Charts with Global Positioning System, 2nd edn. (last accessed June 24, 2008), http://www.geocomm.com/channel/gps/news/nimagps2/
9. NRC: Summary of Workshop on Using Information Technology to Enhance Disaster Management. The National Academics Press, Washington, DC (2005)
10. Palen, L., Hiltz, S.R., Liu, S.: Online Forums Supporting Grassroots Participation in Emergency Preparedness and Response. Communication of the ACM 50(3), 54–58
11. Pitt Review learning Lessons from the 2007 Floods (Interim report), Cabinet Office, London, UK (December 2007)
12. Van Den Eede, G., Van de Walle, B.: Operational risk in incident management: a cross-fertilisation between ISCRAM and IT governance. In: Van de Walle, B., Carle, B. (eds.) Proceedings of the 2nd international conference on information systems for crisis response and management ISCRAM 2005, pp. 53–60 (2005)
13. Waldher, F., Thierry, J., Grasser, S.: Aspects of Anatomical and Chronological Sequence Diagrams in Software-Supported Emergency Care Patient Report Forms. In: Löffler, J., Klann, M. (eds.) Mobile Response 2007. LNCS, vol. 4458, pp. 9–18. Springer, Heidelberg (2007)

Humanitarian Information Management and Systems

Bartel Van de Walle[1], Gerd Van Den Eede[2], and Willem Muhren[1]

[1] Tilburg University, Department of Information Management and Systems,
5000 LE Tilburg, The Netherlands
{bartel,w.j.muhren}@uvt.nl
[2] Hogeschool-Universiteit Brussel, Stormstraat 2, B-1000 Brussels, Belgium
gerd.vandeneede@hubrussel.be

Abstract. In times of major disasters such as hurricane Katrina or the Sichuan earthquake, the need for accurate and timely information is as crucial as is rapid and coherent coordination among the responding humanitarian community. Effective humanitarian information systems that provide timely access to comprehensive, relevant, and reliable information are critical to humanitarian operations. The faster the humanitarian community is able to collect, analyze, disseminate and act on key information, the more effective the response will be, the better needs will be met, and the greater the benefit to the affected populations. This paper presents fundamental principles of humanitarian information management as endorsed by the international humanitarian community, introduces generic systems design premises and presents two recent collaborative efforts in humanitarian information systems development.

Keywords: humanitarian community, UN, OCHA, information management, information systems, SAHANA, IRMA.

1 Introduction

Within the dynamic context of humanitarian operations, the need for timely, relevant and reliable information is widely recognized by the humanitarian actors in the field as well as by the remote headquarters of their organizations. *Information management* covers "the various stages of information processing from production to storage and retrieval to dissemination towards the better working of an organization; information can be from internal and external sources and in any format" (AIM 2005). Increasingly, *information technology* is playing a key role in enabling effective and efficient information management. This, in turn, creates the main challenge of integrating the technology within the established work processes of the humanitarian actors, in order to create – in the terms of Alter (2002) – a *work system*.

A work system is a system in which "human participants and/or machines use information, technologies, and other resources to perform processes for producing products and/or services for internal or external customers" (Alter 2002). *Information systems* then constitute a special case of work systems in which the processes performed and products and services produced are devoted to information. The activities in these processes are limited to six types of computerized or manual activities:

J. Löffler and M. Klann (Eds.): Mobile Response, LNCS 5424, pp. 12–21, 2009.

information capturing, transmitting, storing, retrieving, manipulating and displaying. Information systems consist of information technology (hardware, software, networks) obviously, but also include infrastructure (technical infrastructure such as telecom or even electricity, as well as human infrastructure or people capable of working with the system), participants (those who operate or contribute to the system), processes, and ultimately customers or end-users. In addition to information processing, activities in these larger work systems also include communication, sense making, decision making, thinking and physical action (Alter 2002). Track-and-trace systems for example are information systems, yet the users also take part in a larger work system, for instance sending medical staff and medicine to disaster-stricken areas.

In the following section, we present essential information management principles that have been endorsed by the participants of a major humanitarian information management gathering in Geneva in 2007, as *"a common vision of the central role of information in support of effective humanitarian preparedness, response and recovery"* (Global Symposium+5 Final Report 2008). Section 3 turns to information systems, and we begin this Section by introducing a set of design premises for dynamic emergency response management information systems (DERMIS). We then move on to two state-of-the-art developments, and briefly describe SAHANA, an FOSS (Free and Open Source Software) generic disaster management system and IRMA, a recently funded European research projects involving African partners to create a risk management system for Africa. We conclude in Section 4 with some important observations.

2 Humanitarian Information Management Principles

2.1 UN Office for the Coordination of Humanitarian Affairs

The UN's Office for the Coordination of Humanitarian Affairs (OCHA) was established in 1991 with a specific mandate to work with operational relief agencies to ensure that there are no gaps in the response and that duplication of effort is avoided. OCHA's information management extends from the gathering and collection of information and data, to its integration, analysis, synthesis, and dissemination via the Internet and other means. To respond to information needs, OCHA has developed humanitarian information systems which include ReliefWeb, the regional information networks (IRIN), information management units (IMUs) and humanitarian information centers (HICs). All of these services have established solid reputations in the provision of quality information and are recognized as essential in the coordination of emergency response among partners in the humanitarian community.

Common in the success of these systems, or information services, is that the information provided is based upon a solid information exchange network among all partners in the humanitarian community. *ReliefWeb* (http://www.reliefweb.int) is the world's leading online gateway to information on humanitarian emergencies and disasters. Through ReliefWeb, OCHA provides practitioners with information on both complex emergencies and natural disasters worldwide from over 1,000 sources, including UN, governments, nongovernmental organizations (NGOs), the academic community, and the media. ReliefWeb consolidates final reports, documents, and reports from humanitarian partners, providing a global repository one-stop shop for emergency response information. *IRIN*s gather information from a range of humanitarian and other sources, providing context and reporting on emergencies and at-risk countries. *IMU*s and *HIC*s collect, manage, and disseminate operational data and information at the field level, providing geographic information products and a range of operations databases and related content to decision makers in the field as well as headquarters.

2.2 Global Symposium+5 Humanitarian IM Principles

Representatives of donor agencies, governmental organizations, United Nations agencies, Red Cross Movement, non-governmental organizations (NGOs), scientific and research institutes, academia, the media and private sector met at the Global Symposium +5 in Geneva on 22-26 October 2007, supported by the UN Office for the Coordination of Humanitarian Affairs and funded with the assistance of the Humanitarian Aid Department of the European Commission (ECHO). The Symposium reaffirmed the outcomes of the earlier 2002 Symposium on Best Practices in Humanitarian Information Management and Exchange, in particular the Statement on Best Practices in Humanitarian Information Management and Exchange, as well as recalling the outcomes of the three Humanitarian Information Network (HIN) Workshops held in Bangkok (in 2003), Panama (in 2005), and Nairobi (in 2006).

Symposium participants reviewed and amended the Principles of Humanitarian Information Management and Exchange that were endorsed by the 2002 Symposium to better reflect the humanitarian environment of today. In endorsing the revised principles, the Symposium reiterated the need to develop and encourage accountability in the application of the following humanitarian information management principles (Global Symposium+5 2007).

- *Accessibility*. Humanitarian information and data should be made accessible to all humanitarian actors by applying easy-to-use formats and by translating information into common or local languages. Information and data for humanitarian purposes should be made widely available through a variety of online and offline distribution channels including the media.
- *Inclusiveness*. Information management and exchange should be based on collaboration, partnership and sharing with a high degree of participation and ownership by multiple stakeholders including national and local governments, and especially affected communities whose information needs should equally be taken into account.
- *Inter-operability*. All sharable data and information should be made available in formats that can be easily retrieved, shared and used by humanitarian organizations.
- *Accountability*. Information providers should be responsible to their partners and stakeholders for the content they publish and disseminate.
- *Verifiability*. Information should be accurate, consistent and based on sound methodologies, validated by external sources, and analyzed within the proper contextual framework.
- *Relevance*. Information should be practical, flexible, responsive, and driven by operational needs in support of decision-making throughout all phases of a crisis. Data that is not relevant should not be collected.

- *Impartiality.* Information managers should consult a variety of sources when collecting and analyzing information so as to provide varied and balanced perspectives for addressing problems and recommending solutions.
- *Humanity.* Information should never be used to distort, to mislead or to cause harm to affected or at risk populations and should respect the dignity of victims.
- *Timeliness.* Humanitarian information should be collected, analyzed and disseminated efficiently, and must be kept current.
- *Sustainability.* Humanitarian information and data should be preserved, cataloged and archived, so that it can be retrieved for future use, such as for preparedness, analysis, lessons learned and evaluation. The use of Open Source Software should be promoted to further enhance access to information by all stakeholders in a sustainable way. When possible, post emergency data should be transitioned to relevant recovery actors and host governments and training provided on its use.

In addition, the Global Symposium+5 added three new Principles:

- *Reliability.* Users must be able to evaluate the reliability and credibility of data and information by knowing its source and method of collection. Collection methods should adhere to global standards where they exist to support and reinforce credibility. Reliability is a prerequisite for ensuring validity and verifiability.
- *Reciprocity.* Information exchange should be a beneficial two-way process between the affected communities and the humanitarian community, including affected governments.
- *Confidentiality.* The processing of any personal data shall not be done without the prior explicit description of its purpose and will only be done for that purpose, and after prior informed consent of the individual concerned. Sufficient safeguards must be put in place to protect personal data against loss, unauthorized processing and other misuse. If sensitive information is publicly disclosed, the sources of such information will not be released when there is a reasonable risk that doing so will affect the security or integrity of these sources.

The participants at the Global Symposium+5 endorsed these Principles and issued a Symposium Final Statement expressing a common vision of the central role of information in support of effective humanitarian preparedness, response and recovery. They also agreed on the need to strengthen the existing community of practice on humanitarian information, the Humanitarian Information Network (HIN), expanding its membership and building upon its work to date.

3 Humanitarian Information Systems

3.1 Information Systems Design Premises

As argued above, information systems are specific instances of work systems, in which the processes performed and products and services produced are devoted to information (Alter 2002). Weick noted that the ways in which Information Systems (IS) are designed do not really support how people make sense of their environment:

"The problem with IS is that representations in the electronic world can become chaotic for at least two reasons; The data in these representations are flawed, and the people who manage those flawed data have limited processing capacity. These two problems interact in a potentially deadly vicious circle. The data are flawed because they are incomplete; they contain only what can be collected and processed through machines. That excludes sensory information, feelings, intuitions, and context — all of which are necessary for an accurate perception of what is happening. Feelings, context, and sensory information are not soft-headed luxuries. They are ways of knowing that preserve properties of events not captured by machine-compatible information. To withhold these incompatible data is to handicap the observer. And therein lies the problem." (Weick, 1985, p. 51-52).

In a seminal paper on the design of Dynamic Emergency Response Management Information Systems (DERMIS), Turoff and co-workers outlined nine fundamental design premises (Turoff et al. 2004). The nine premises and their underlying objectives and requirements cut across all types of crisis and emergency situations, and hold no presumption as to whether the system is intended to deal with natural disasters, man-made or industrial disasters, or humanitarian disasters. It is precisely the lack of dependency upon specified content that makes an emergency response system a powerful tool to apply to any emergency once the users have had the training and experience to master it. There may be supporting data bases that contain content information such as the location and availability of specific resources for specific types of crisis situations or information and knowledge about such things as hazardous materials. These database resources could be anywhere, it is only necessary that the local responders know about them and how to be able to use them if needed. Turoff et al. conclude that "the system that carries out the response and allows the humans involved to coordinate and exercise various levels of command and control *has to be a communication system tailored for the emergency response mission*". The nine design premises are (Turoff et al. 2004):

1. **System Training and Simulation:** An emergency system that is not used on a regular basis before an emergency will never be of use in an actual emergency.
2. **Information Focus:** People responding to an emergency are working 14-18 hour days and have no tolerance or time for things unrelated to dealing with the crisis.
3. **Crisis Memory:** Learning and understanding what actually happened before, during, and after the crisis is extremely important for the improvement of the response process.
4. **Exceptions as Norms:** Almost everything in a crisis is an exception to the norm.
5. **Scope and Nature of Crisis:** The critical problem of the moment is the nature of the crisis, a primary factor requiring people, authority, and resources to be brought together at a specific period of time for a specific purpose.
6. **Role Transferability:** It is impossible to predict who will undertake what specific role in a crisis situation. The actions and privileges of the role need to be well defined in the software of the system and people must be trained for the possibility of assuming multiple or changing roles.
7. **Information Validity and Timeliness:** Establishing and supporting confidence in a decision by supplying the best possible up-to-date information is critical to those whose actions may risk lives and resources.

8. **Free Exchange of Information:** Crises involve the necessity for many hundreds of individuals from different organizations to be able to freely exchange information, delegate authority, and conduct oversight, without the side effect of information overload.

9. **Coordination:** The crux of the coordination problem for large crisis response groups is that the exact actions and responsibilities of the individuals cannot be pre-determined.

3.2 Free and Open Source Software for Crisis Management: SAHANA

Very few countries and organizations commit sufficient resources to disaster management, regardless of past experience or potential future. Disaster management becomes a pressing concern only after the disaster has struck – a concern which may be short-lived, as other needs quickly surface again. While this is obviously true of poorer developing nations, it is also often the case in richer developed countries; there are always higher priority projects that need funding, and investment in disaster preparedness remains low around the world.

As the issues addressed by disaster management systems are relevant for any country dealing with a disaster, ideally such systems should be shared, developed and owned globally. The Free and Open Source Software (FOSS) development and community mechanisms have a proven track record in building such systems. In particular, we believe that the FOSS principles and practice mesh well with the humanitarian sector on three important criteria (Currion et al., 2006):

1. **Approach:** The FOSS approach, i.e. an open, transparent and grassroots shared movement, fits very well with the proclaimed principles of most humanitarian organizations.

2. **Cost:** Although there is an initial cost in setting up a FOSS disaster management system in terms of technical support, the system is no-cost to procure and low-cost to maintain. This overcomes some of the basic resource constraints that affect many governmental and non-governmental organizations. This particularly addresses the problem of lack of funding before a disaster strikes or any administrative constraints that would require a long procurement process for a high-cost license. In addition, FOSS development leverages the goodwill and expertise of a global community of IT and non-IT actors at no cost.

3. **Adaptability:** The approach and cost factors described above combine to make it possible for a FOSS disaster management system to be set up, adapted and localized quickly, so that it can be more responsive to the specific situation. Since it is FOSS, the source code is available for anybody to adapt freely; as a web-based system, it does not require end users to install additional software and updates can be managed centrally.

SAHANA is a web based collaboration tool that addresses the common coordination problems during a disaster from finding missing people, managing aid, managing volunteers, tracking relocation sites, etc. between government, the civil society (NGOs) and the victims themselves. Sahana is an integrated set of pluggable, web based disaster management applications that provide solutions to large-scale humanitarian problems in the aftermath of a disaster. The main applications and problems they address are as follows:

- **Missing Person Registry:** helping to reduce trauma by effectively finding missing persons;
- **Organization Registry:** coordinating and balancing the distribution of relief organizations in the affected areas and connecting relief groups, allowing them to operate as one;
- **Request Management System:** registering and tracking all incoming requests for support and relief up to fulfillment and helping donors connect to relief requirements;
- **Camp Registry:** tracking the location and numbers of victims in the various camps and temporary shelters set up all around the affected area.

The development of Sahana, a Free and Open Source Disaster Management system distributed under terms of the GNU Lesser General Public License, was triggered by the Tsunami disaster in 2004 to help coordinate the relief effort in Sri Lanka (Sahana 2006). It was initially built by a group of volunteers from the Sri Lankan IT industry and spearheaded by Lanka Software Foundation. An implementation of Sahana was authorized and deployed by CNO (the main government body in Sri Lanka coordinating the relief effort) to help coordinate all the data being captured. Development of Sahana continues today to make the system applicable for global use and to be able to handle any large scale disaster. Sahana has been deployed successfully in the aftermath of several large natural disasters, for instance following the large earthquake in Pakistan in 2005, and the mudslide disaster in the Philippines and the Yogjakarta earthquake, both in 2006. The long term objectives of Sahana are to grow into a complete disaster management system, including functionality for mitigation, preparation, relief and recovery. The current status, ongoing development and future goals are intensively discussed in two web-based communities, the Sahana wiki pages (Sahana 2006) and the Humanitarian-ICT Yahoo! Group (Humanitarian-ICT 2006).

3.3 IRMA

IRMA (short for Integrated Risk Management for Africa) is a recently funded European research project involving research groups from Europe and Africa (IRMA 2008). The purpose of the IRMA project is to build a reference platform suitable for the management of natural and environmental risks in Africa. The platform must allow the stakeholders in risks management to develop and use tailored risk management models; therefore, the platform will provide similar facilities as earlier European IT-based risk management projects, and should make it easy to allow for multi-risk management, i.e. the platform will exploit the commonalities of the information sources and take into account the interdependencies between different hazards.

The IRMA platform will feature two major technical components:

- an environment for providing services of all kinds related to the acquisition, processing, dissemination of information and an efficient storage of all relevant information so that the stakeholders can analyze afterwards the sequence of events and adapt operational procedures consequently, and

- a multi-purpose solution for the communications (sensor networks, remote sensed data transfer, service access, alert, emergency communications)

The project has the following key objectives:

- IRMA will develop and demonstrate a truly multi-risk approach that takes into account the systemic nature of environmental risks, such as: consistent multiple risk mapping, decision support. The concept of multi-hazard approach has been debated in various international events, however the concept needs to be further explored, implemented and demonstrated to understand the achievable benefit of this new approach and its implications on organizational and operational aspects.
- The project will address the availability and reliability of a defined collection of ubiquitous services and existing networks including POTS ensuring public safety communication on critical infrastructures by leveraging redundant communication channels wherever possible and using automatic redirection or transformation of communications in case of network failures. The main focus will be on the network layer i.e. on "bridging" networks using the Internet Protocol (IP), with particular emphasis on leveraging IP version 6 (IPv6) as an enabler for providing the new functionalities. Existing and future crisis handling middleware will be interfaced by using open standard network interfaces.
- The problem of identification will be addressed by adapting new research results in the area of wireless and ad hoc networks, where especially the integration of distributed knowledge of the current network environment (location information, redundancy, RFID messages, recommended trust relations, etc.) into the protocols will be a key issue for context adaptable recognition. With IPv6 (and mobile, ad hoc solutions) there already exists a platform for feasibility analyses and implementation tests, which could solve dependability demands for fixed as well as for mobile and POTS technologies.
- The project will integrate existing services in an open Service Oriented Architecture which is compliant with EU SDI (INSPIRE) and UNSDI. To this end, the consortium will re-use the results of previous integrated projects such as WIN and ORCHESTRA.
- The project will apply the S&T research results to practical reference scenarios to check against the models and to quantify the improvements. The results will be demonstrated in scenarios involving different hazards in Cameroon, Senegal, Mozambique and South Africa.
- The Platform developed in the project will use the results of previous research projects funded by the EU and will be compatible with parallel developments such as GMES, GEOSS.
- The Platform developed in the project will allow the stakeholders in Africa to develop their own approach for the risk management (models, data sources, response process, etc).

The IRMA project intends to offer a technical solution for multi-risks management in Africa, which will have the following major characteristics.

(1) Provide Tools, Standards and Processes benefiting from the latest development in IT for Environment and Risk Management, in order to:

- build generic platforms serving multiple purpose, beyond the initial scope of Risk Management;
- support the easy and cost effective development and implementation of risk management applications;
- provide innovative User Interface features more friendly with African culture.

(2) Implement Data Communications over existing or easy-to-deploy communications facilities, which comprise Internet, satellite link and Wireless.

(3) Take into account all possible sources of information that are available at economically affordable conditions, in order to avoid duplication of efforts and costs and compensate for limited data acquisition capabilities.

4 Conclusion

Information management is today widely recognized in the humanitarian community as fundamental yet extremely delicate. The information that is being collected, processed and analyzed may indeed contribute to improve the livelihoods of people affected by a disaster, but can also endanger the lives of those people, if the information is inadequate, misleading or gets in the hands of malevolent groups. Information professionals in the humanitarian community have therefore formulated a number of basic principles, which amplify the central role of information for effective humanitarian action. The information systems that are built to support these information processes must take these principles into account, so that they effectively support humanitarian work processes. The two recent developments of Sahana and Irma serve as an illustration of the growing efforts of the humanitarian community and academic research groups worldwide to work in partnership and build information systems that accomplish this goal.

Acknowledgments. The authors are grateful to Jobst Loffler and Markus Klann for their interest in this work. Research support from the Crisis Management Initiative (CMI) in Finland is gratefully acknowledged, as is funding provided by the Interactive Collaborative Information Systems (ICIS) project (http://www.icis.decis.nl/), supported by the Dutch Ministry of Economic Affairs, grant nr: BSIK03024.

References

1. AIM, Association for Information Management website (last accessed July 16, 2007), http://www.aslib.co.uk
2. Alter, S.: The Work Systems Method for Understanding Information Systems and Information Systems Research. Communications of the AIS 9, 90–104 (2002)
3. Belardo, S., Harrald, J.: A framework for the application of decision support systems to the problem of planning for catastrophic events. IEEE transactions on Engineering Management 39(4), 400–411 (1992)
4. Currion, P.: Report on Information and Technology Requirements, Emergency Capacity Building Project. In: CARE 2006 (2006)
5. Currion, P., de Silva, C., Van de Walle, B.: Open Source Software for Disaster Management. Communications of the ACM 50(3), 61–65 (2007)

6. de Silva, C.: Sahana FOSS disaster management system. In: Hoe, N.S. (ed.) Breaking Barriers: The Potential of Free and Open Source Software for Sustainable Human Development - A Compilation of Case Studies from Across the World, United Nations Development Programme UNDP-APDIP, pp. 55–61. Elsevier, Amsterdam (2006)
7. Haggerty, A. (ed.): Global Symposium+5 Final Report, Information for Humanitarian Action. UN OCHA, Geneva (2008)
8. Hale, J.: A layered communication architecture for the support of crisis response. Journal of Management Information Systems 14(1), 235–255 (summer 1997)
9. IRMA, Integrated Risk Management for Africa, EU 7th Framework Programme, Theme ICT-2007.6.3, ICT for Environmental Management and Energy Efficiency. STREP grant agreement 224353 (2008)
10. Muhren, W.J., Van Den Eede, G., Van de Walle, B.: Sensemaking and implications for information systems design: Findings from the Democratic Republic of Congo's ongoing crisis. Information Technology for Development 14(3), 197–212 (2008)
11. Turoff, M.: Past and Future Emergency Response Information Systems. Communications of the ACM 45(4), 29–33 (2002)
12. Turoff, M., Chumer, M., Van de Walle, B., Xiang, Y.: The Design of a Dynamic Emergency Response Management Information Systems. Journal of Information Technology Theory and Application 5(4), 1–35 (2004)
13. Van de Walle, B., Turoff, M.: Emergency response information systems: Emerging trends and technologies. Communications of the ACM 50(3), 29–31 (2007)
14. Van de Walle, B., Turoff, M.: Decision support for emergency situations. In: Burstein, F., Holsapple, C. (eds.) Handbook on Decision Support Systems, pp. 39–64. Springer, Heidelberg (2008)
15. Van de Walle, B., Hiltz, S.R., Turoff, M. (eds.): Advances in Management Information Systems Monograph on Information Systems for Crisis Management. Sharpe Publishing, USA (forthcoming, 2009)
16. Weick, K.E.: Cosmos vs. chaos: Sense and nonsense in electronic contexts. Organizational Dynamics 14(2), 51–64 (1985)

A Mobile RFID-Based System for Supporting Evacuation of Buildings

Luca Chittaro and Daniele Nadalutti

HCI Lab
Dept. of Math and Computer Science
University of Udine
via delle Scienze, 206
33100 Udine, Italy
{chittaro,daniele.nadalutti}@dimi.uniud.it

Abstract. Natural and man-made disasters present the need to efficiently and effectively evacuate the people occupying the affected buildings. In such situations, people are usually under stress and the use of a location-aware mobile application for giving evacuation instructions in simple and effective ways can be useful to improve users' decision making. This paper proposes a mobile system that gives evacuation instructions by employing an interactive 3D location-aware model of the building. The main focus of the paper is on the solutions and the technologies adopted for determining user's position into the building and for interactively visualizing a 3D model of the building augmented with visual evacuation instructions on mobile devices.

1   Introduction

Natural and man-made disasters present the need to efficiently and effectively evacuate the people occupying the affected buildings. The occupants have to be evacuated as soon as possible (e.g., in case of fire) or immediately after the event (e.g., in case of earthquake). Considering the complexity of large buildings and the possible large number of occupants, it is often difficult to organize a quick evacuation, especially when the building is seriously damaged [1]. Moreover, people in a disaster are usually under stress and may "freeze", leading to fatalities in otherwise survivable conditions [2]. Finally, in large public buildings like airports, the occupants can also be unaware of the topology of the building or the location of the emergency exits and they are usually not trained in evacuating such buildings.

A location-aware mobile application for giving evacuation instructions in simple and effective ways can be useful to improve users' decision making, preventing users' errors and minimizing casualties. Moreover, location-aware mobile applications can be used for training purposes, providing the user with emergency simulations, so that she can learn evacuation paths for different scenarios by actually following them in the building to gain knowledge and abilities that will

J. Löffler and M. Klann (Eds.): Mobile Response, LNCS 5424, pp. 22–31, 2009.

be useful in real emergencies. Moreover, users' actions can be logged by the application for post-training analysis.

It must be noticed that distasters often cause power outages in the affected building. For this reason, the technologies (e.g., wireless networks) adopted by the mobile application (e.g., for positioning) should not require availability of electrical power in the building to work properly.

This paper proposes a mobile system that uses 3D models of the building for giving evacuation instructions to the user. The system employs a mobile 3D rendering engine [3] to interactively visualize a location-aware 3D model of the building augmented with visual evacuation instructions. User's position into the building is determined by using active short-range RFID technology without the need for an electrical network. The system supports also manual navigation of the model for training purposes or if automatic positioning is not available.

The paper is organized as follows. Section 2 will briefly discuss related work. Section 3 will describe our system, analyzing its components and motivating the major design choices. Section 4 will provide conclusions and outline future work directions.

2   Related Work

A location-aware mobile system to support occupants' evacuation needs to rely on an appropriate positioning technology and to present navigation instructions in an easy-to-understand way.

Several technologies can be employed for indoor positioning (e.g, Infrared, indoor GPS, RFID, UWB, GSM, WLAN, Bluetooth, UHF, Ultrasound). Liu et al. [4] present a survey of wireless indoor positioning systems. They compare performance of several approaches in terms of accuracy, precision, robustness, scalability, complexity and cost.

Two well-known indoor localization systems (SpotON [5] and LANDMARC [6]) are based on active RFID technology. Both systems track the position of a specified tag by measuring its distance from multiple RFID readers that are placed at specific locations. The distance between a tag and a reader is computed based on received signal strength. To increase accuracy without placing more RFID readers, the LANDMARC system also uses a set of RFID tags, called reference tags, that are placed at fixed locations and serve as reference point for the system. The position of the tracked tag is computed as the weighted average of the positions of the k nearest reference tags, where weighting factors are based on estimated distances between the tracked tag and the k reference tags. However, these solutions for indoor localization based on RFID technology are not suitable for mobile emergency applications because they need a network to allow the communication between each RFID reader and a server where the position of the tracked tag is computed. Moreover, a wireless network is also needed for sending the computed position back to the mobile device. An alternative approach, less accurate but more suited to emergency situations, consists in using a single mobile RFID reader (e.g., Compact Flash RFID reader) on the mobile device and a set of tags that are placed at fixed locations: the mobile device can autonomously compute its position based only on distance between the reader and the tags without the need for network infrastructure.

Presentation of navigation instructions on mobile devices is a widely discussed topic in the literature. Baus et al. [7] surveyed the different solutions employed in mobile guides, especially for tourists. Most existing solutions are based on 2D maps, but alternative approaches have been studied, such as photos of the environment augmented with visual navigation aids (e.g., arrows); 3D models; textual instructions; audio directions; route sketches. Approaches based on 2D maps have the advantage of exploiting a well-known method for representing spatial information, but 3D models or augmented photos exploit natural users' spatial abilities because they provide users with the same visual cues they exploit in the real world (e.g., occlusion, size of the objects). Moreover, solutions based on 3D models might allow the user to train in navigating a building without being in it. However, using 3D graphics on mobile devices for navigation purposes is currently a scarcely explored subject in the literature. The first investigations were thought for outdoor environments [8, 9]. Later, some projects explored the use of 3D models for helping users in the navigation of indoor environments [10]. Garcia Barbosa et al. [10] developed a framework which allows users to load 3D models from a remote PC server, navigate them, find an optimal and collision-free path from one place to another, and obtain additional information on objects. A significant limitation of the framework is the lack of automatic positioning: the user has to navigate the model manually. Moreover, the employed 3D models are very simple and this could make it difficult for users to visually match them with the real world. Finally, the framework needs a wireless network infrastructure to compute paths.

In recent years, only a few attempts have been made at exploring the use of 3D graphics on mobile devices for presenting evacuation instructions. Garcia Barbosa et al. [10] considered the application of their framework for virtual rescue training of firefighters. Pu and Zlatanova [1] list instead the requirements for a mobile system and a framework to manage evacuation of buildings using 3D models, but they do not implement it.

3   The Proposed System

To the best of our knowledge, our system is the first mobile system that uses location-aware 3D models of buildings for evacuation purposes. The system represents paths by means of a set of bidimensional oriented arrows that are projected on the floor. Emergency exits are highlighted by using spotlights [11] (Figure 1).

The system uses a single compact flash RFID reader on the mobile device and a set of tags placed at fixed locations to determine user's position in the building and to consequently update the position and the orientation of the viewpoint in the 3D model. As it is typical of navigators, there are some limitations in determining user's orientation. The system, indeed, computes user's orientation from

Fig. 1. A 3D model augmented with evacuation instructions. Paths are represented by arrows (left figure), while landmarks are highlighted by spotlights (right figure).

her latest positions, so if the user makes a turn without significantly changing her position in the world, the system is not able to recognize the change of orientation. Inaccurate computed orientations can lead to wrong and useless viewpoints in the 3D model (e.g., a viewpoint that is very close to a wall and orientated towards the wall), with consequent difficulties for users to match their position in the real world with the 3D world. To avoid this, we adopt a solution inspired by car navigators and we snap user's positions and orientations to the evacuation path.

3.1 Architecture and Functions

Figure 2 illustrates the architecture of the proposed system, composed by three main modules: the *Viewpoint Calculator*, the *Path Planner*, and the *MobiX3D Viewer*.

The Viewpoint Calculator reads the queue of detected tags from the RFID reader, retrieves their coordinates in the real world from the Tag Positions database, and then computes the user's current position and her orientation. Finally, it sends the corresponding position and orientation of the viewpoint in the 3D model to the Path Planner. We use a reader for Beacon RFID tags, i.e. active tags that periodically send a signal to the reader. The specific tags we use have a range of about 4 meters and send their signal to the reader every 500 milliseconds. The RFID reader simply stores the detected tags in a queue that is queried by the Viewpoint Calculator every 500 milliseconds.

The Viewpoint Calculator then computes position and orientation of the viewpoint in four steps: (i) computation of a rough viewpoint position (i.e., a position

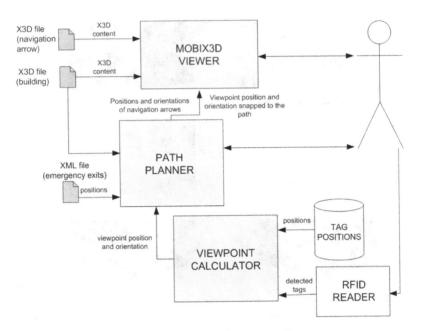

Fig. 2. Architecture of the proposed system

derived by triangulating the detected RFID tags), (ii) computation of current viewpoint position by filtering the latest rough viewpoint positions, (iii) computation of rough viewpoint orientation from the latest two current viewpoint positions, (iv) computation of current viewpoint orientation by filtering the latest rough viewpoint orientations.

In the first step, the Viewpoint Calculator computes a rough viewpoint position by using a simple algorithm based on detected tags and on the strength of their signal. For each detected tag, the algorithm estimates the distance d from the tag based on signal strength (which decreases exponentially as one moves away from the tag) and is computed using the following formula [12]:

$$d = 10^{\frac{(P_0 - P(d))}{10n}}$$

where P_0 is the signal strength at 1 m, $P(d)$ is the signal strength at distance d, n is a constant that determines how the signal strength decreases as the distance increases and has to be tuned empirically. In our tests, n has be tuned to the behavior of the specific tags and reader we employ (and is equal to 2.4967854). However, if the signal strength associated to a tag is over a certain threshold, which corresponds to the typical strength obtained when the reader is very close (< 50 cm) to a tag, then we set d equal to 0.5 m. The rough viewpoint position is computed by using triangulation. When no tags are detected, the rough viewpoint position that is generated is the one computed 500 milliseconds before. For this reason, the computed viewpoint in the 3D model might at times suffer from slight delays in update. In extreme cases, if no tags are detected for a minute, the system warns that the viewpoint in the 3D model could not be in sync with the actual position of the user.

In the second step, the Viewpoint Calculator computes the current viewpoint position, i.e. the position sent to the Path Planner, by filtering the latest rough viewpoint positions. We currently use a simple filter that computes the mean of the latest 5 rough viewpoint positions. In the first 2 seconds, when less than 5 rough viewpoint positions are available, the mean is computed considering the available rough viewpoint positions.

In the third step, the Viewpoint Calculator computes a rough viewpoint orientation as the vector between the latest two viewpoint positions.

In the fourth step, the Viewpoint Calculator computes the current viewpoint orientation, i.e. the orientation sent to the MobiX3D viewer, by filtering the latest rough viewpoint orientations in the same way of the positions. The Viewpoint Calculator sends current viewpoint position and orientation to the Path Planner every 500 milliseconds.

The Path Planner has two main functions: (i) computing the evacuation path from current position to the nearest emergency exit, and (ii) snapping position and orientation of the viewpoint computed by the Viewpoint Calculator into the current path. To compute evacuation paths, the Path Planner uses current viewpoint position and orientation, a 2D map of the building (derived from the 3D model) and the position of the emergency exits. The evacuation path is represented as a directed acyclic graph G where each node is associated to a waypoint and two consecutive waypoints are connected by an edge. Formally, $G = (V, E)$, where $V = \{v_0, \ldots, v_{n-1}\}$, $v_i = (x_i, y_i, z_i)$ is a point in space, v_0 is located at the current position, and v_{n-1} is located at the nearest emergency exit. E is defined as follows:

$$E = \{(v_i, v_j) | v_i, v_j \in V, i = \{0, \ldots, n-2\}, j = i+1\}$$

For each edge, the Path Planner sends to the MobiX3D Viewer the position and the orientation of a navigation arrow. The position of the i-th navigation arrow is the mean of of v_i and v_{i+1}, while its orientation is the unit vector pointing from v_i towards v_{i+1}.

To snap the position and the orientation of the viewpoint to the evacuation path, the Path Planner locates the node v_j of the evacuation path nearest to the viewpoint and sends the coordinates of v_j as viewpoint position and the unit vector pointing from v_j towards v_{j+1} as viewpoint orientation to the MobiX3D Viewer.

The MobiX3D Viewer displays the 3D model of the building augmented with the evacuation arrows. It also allows the user to switch among automatic and manual navigation modes. Automatic navigation mode updates the viewpoint in the 3D model based on viewpoint positions and orientations sent by the Path Planner. Manual navigation mode allows the user to navigate the model by pressing the cursor keys of the mobile device. It is useful for training purposes or if no RFID tags are available. The input of the MobiX3D Viewer is the model of the building, the position and the orientation of the viewpoint in the 3D world, the model of the navigation arrows, their position and their orientation. The Mo-biX3D Viewer was originally proposed in [3] as a general X3D file viewer and was later refined [13] with a basic view frustum culling algorithm and extended with a portal culling algorithm [14] for buildings. The portal culling extension is used for very large buildings, when the entire 3D model cannot be loaded in memory. To test the evacuation system, we used a model of our Department, made of 50.000 triangles. The size of the source file is 4.38 MB, with 100 kB of textures, and can be loaded in memory without using the portal culling extension.

3.2   Tests on Tag Availability

We tested the system positioning algorithm on three different tag setups: (i) 4 tags placed about 8 m away from each other in a 24 meter corridor, (ii) 4 tags placed on the vertices of a 4-meter square, and (iii) 9 tags placed on a 4-meter square, following a regular 3x3 grid pattern (the 4-meter square was divided into four 2-meters squares).

We performed a walk along the corridor at a constant speed in the first setup, and a walk into the square following random trajectories at a constant speed in the second and the third setups. No other people were in the areas where tests were performed. The system logged the number of detected tags each time it sent a rough viewpoint position to the filter (i.e., every 500 milliseconds).

In the first setup, no tags were detected 49% of times when a rough viewpoint position was sent to the filter, 1 tag was detected 42% of times, and more than 1 tag was detected 9% of times. In the second setup, no tags were detected 7% of times, 1 tag was detected 46% of times, and more than one tag was detected 47% of times. Finally, in the third setup, no tags were detected 3% of times, 1 tag was detected 6% of times, and more than 1 tag was detected 91% of times.

Although the percentage of tag detection in the first setup was not high, it caused only an intermittent and slight delay in viewpoint updating, and one could easily match the current position in the real world with the position of the viewpoint in the 3D model. However, the second and the third setups guaranteed a higher refresh rate of the viewpoint, allowing for more immediate matching of movements in the real world with viewpoint changes.

3.3   Accuracy and Precision

We preliminary measured the accuracy and the precision of our positioning algorithm by following the methodology described in [15]. We used the metric error distance, i.e., the spatial distance between the real position and the position computed by our positioning algorithm.

We carried out two tests. In the first one, we employed the third tag setup described in Section 3.2. We randomly chose a number of positions in the square and placed the mobile device equipped with the RFID reader at such positions. The mobile device remained in each position for 15 seconds (30 current viewpoint positions were computed) before moving to another position. The accuracy in terms of mean distance error was 0.8 m, with a precision of 90% within 1.5 m.

In the second test, we employed the first tag setup described in Section 3.2. We walked along the corridor at a constant speed for a number of times and the walking speed varied among the different walks. We measured an accuracy of 2 m in terms of mean distance error, with a precision of 75% within 3 m.

3.4 Placing Tags in the Building

Placement of tags in the building is a crucial aspect for the accuracy of positioning. An optimal placement guarantees the full coverage of the building by using the minimum number of tags without losing accuracy. This problem is considered by the EasyReader visual tool [16] for placing RFID tags, antennas and interrogators. The tool provides the user with a 2D visual map of the floors of the building and allows the user to drag and drop RFID components into the 2D map and visually show the coverage. Once the user places the components in a satisfactory way, the tool automatically generates a bill of materials for deployment and installation. However, that tool is aimed at designing configurations of RFID readers placed at fixed locations and used to track the position of moving RFID tags.

We instead developed a visual tool, called TagPlacer that: (i) is aimed at configurations of tags (to be placed at fixed locations) that will be read by a single mobile RFID reader, and (ii) employs 3D models of buildings to facilitate the design. The tool helps the designer to quickly place tags in the building (Figure 3) by navigating the model and placing tags around. The tags are represented by black boxes labeled with red texts that indicate the tag ID. Moreover, spheres that represent the coverage of each tag can be displayed, so one can easily check whether there are uncovered areas or large overlaps among coverages of different

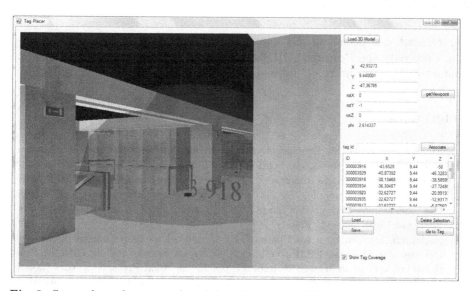

Fig. 3. Screenshot of our visual tool for placing tags. Each semitransparent sphere represents the coverage of the RFID tag.

tags in the part of building she would like to cover. Finally, one can directly store the associations between positions and tag IDs in a Tag Positions database (Figure 2) which is then used by our mobile application, and can load and edit other existing Tag Position databases.

4   Conclusions and Future Work

The system has been informally evaluated on 11 users in our Department with positive results that are described in a companion paper [17]. After focusing mainly on positioning and navigation support, our research is now proceeding in several directions. Firstly, we will improve the computation of the evacuation path, allowing the user to avoid the parts of the building that are damaged and unaccessible. This feature is crucial for evacuation purposes because the shortest path can cross areas of the building which have become dangerous. Some techniques have been proposed to efficiently compute the evacuation path with those additional constraints [1]. Then, we will improve the Tag Placer tool with automatic suggestion of optimal tag placements that cover the building. Algorithms for optimally placing RFID readers in traditional configurations with multiple RFID readers at fixed positions [18] can be a source of inspiration. Moreover, we will develop a mobile extension of the tool for helping the user in placing RFID tags on the field. Finally, we will consider the status of the battery of the mobile device to influence rendering accuracy and viewpoint updating frequency.

Acknowledgments

Our research has been partially supported by the Italian Ministry of Education, University and Research (MIUR) under the PRIN 2005 project "Adaptive, Context-aware, Multimedia Guides on Mobile Devices".

References

[1] Pu, S., Zlatanova, S.: Evacuation route calculation of inner buildings. In: van Oosterom, P., Zlatanova, S., Fendel, E.M. (eds.) Geo-Information for Disaster Management, Berlin, Germany, pp. 1143–1161. Springer, Heidelberg (2005)

[2] Leach, J.: Why people 'freeze' in an emergency: Temporal and cognitive constraints on survival responses. Aviation, Space, and Environmental Medicine 75(6), 539–542 (2004)

[3] Nadalutti, D., Chittaro, L., Buttussi, F.: Rendering of X3D Content on Mobile Devices with OpenGL ES. In: Web3D 2006: Proceedings of the eleventh international conference on 3D web technology, pp. 19–26. ACM Press, New York (2006)

[4] Liu, H., Darabi, H., Banerjee, P., Liu, J.: Survey of wireless indoor positioning techniques and systems. IEEE Transactions on Systems, Man, and Cybernetics, Part C: Applications and Reviews 37(6), 1067–1080 (2007)

[5] Hightower, J., Want, R., Borriello, G.: SpotON: An indoor 3D location sensing technology based on RF signal strength. Univ. Washington, Seattle, Tech. Rep. UW CSE 2002-02-02 (2000)

[6] Ni, L.M., Liu, Y., Lau, Y.C., Patil, A.P.: LANDMARC: Indoor location sensing using active RFID. Wireless Networks 10(6), 701–710 (2004)

[7] Baus, J., Cheverst, K., Kray, C.: A survey of map-based mobile guides. In: Meng, L., Zipf, A., Reichenbacher, T. (eds.) Map-based mobile services – Theories, Methods and Implementations, Berlin, Germany, pp. 197–216. Springer, Heidelberg (2005)

[8] Rakkolainen, I., Vainio, T.: A 3D City Info for mobile users. Computers & Graphics 25(4), 619–625 (2001)

[9] Laakso, K., Gjesdal, O., Sulebak, J.: Tourist information and navigation support by using 3D maps displayed on mobile devices. In: Proceedings of Mobile HCI Workshop on HCI in Mobile Guides, pp. 34–39 (2003)

[10] Garcia Barbosa, R., Formico Rodrigues, M.A.: Supporting guided navigation in mobile virtual environments. In: VRST 2006: Proceedings of the ACM symposium on Virtual reality software and technology, pp. 220–226. ACM, New York (2006)

[11] Brusilovsky, P.: Adaptive navigation support: From adaptive hypermedia to the adaptive web and beyond. PsychNology Journal 2(1), 7–23 (2004)

[12] Hallberg, J., Nilsson, M.: Positioning with Bluetooth, IrDA and RFID. Lulea University of Technology, MSc. Thesis (2002)

[13] HCI Lab – University of Udine: MobiX3D website (2006), http://hcilab.uniud.it/MobiX3D

[14] Mulloni, A., Nadalutti, D., Chittaro, L.: Interactive walkthrough of large 3d models of buildings on mobile devices. In: Web3D 2007: Proceedings of the twelfth international conference on 3D web technology, pp. 17–25. ACM Press, New York (2007)

[15] Xiang, Z., Song, S., Chen, J., Wang, H., Huang, J., Gao, X.: A wireless LAN based indoor positioning technology. IBM Journal of Research and Development 48(5), 617–626 (2004)

[16] ODIN Technologies, Inc.: EasyReader (2006), http://www.odintechnologies.com/index.php/software/easyreader

[17] Chittaro, L., Nadalutti, D.: Presenting evacuation instructions on mobile devices by means of location-aware 3d virtual environments. In: MobileHCI 2008: Proceedings of the 10th conference on Human-computer interaction with mobile devices and services. ACM Press, New York (2008)

[18] Wang, L., Norman, B., Rajgopal, J.: Placement of multiple RFID reader antennas to maximise portal read accuracy. International Journal of Radio Frequency Identification Technology and Applications 1(3), 260–277 (2007)

Improving Participation, Accessibility and Compliance for Campus-Wide Mobile Emergency Alerting Systems

Helen T. Sullivan[1], Markku T. Häkkinen[2], and Dana Piechocinski[1]

[1] Department of Psychology, Rider University, Lawrenceville, New Jersey, USA
[2] Department of Computer Science and Information Systems,
University of Jyväskylä, Jyväskylä, Finland
{hsullivan,piechocinski}@rider.edu, mhakkinen@acm.org

Abstract. University campus communities face a variety of hazards, from natural and technological disasters to terrorism and violence. In response to recent events, many campuses within the United States have begun to implement emergency notification systems utilizing email, text, and telephone-based messaging. These alerts are designed to reach members of the campus community, including faculty, staff, and students and most rely upon an opt-in model for participation. The present design of both the registration process and the notification messages raise several concerns as to the effectiveness of notification systems. This research presents findings from an examination of emergency notification systems on one campus and discusses approaches to improve such systems for all members of the campus population.

Keywords: Emergency Notifications, Accessibility, Mobile Alerts, Mobile Devices.

1 Introduction

Events ranging from Hurricane Katrina to the Virginia Tech shooting tragedy in 2007 have prompted colleges and universities to adopt or enhance campus emergency notification systems. Short-comings of existing systems, including the one in use at Virginia Tech, have led to calls for improvements in the notification process. Legislation has been enacted at the state level in Virginia requiring that educational institutions adopt emergency notification systems, and national legislation has been proposed that has specific performance requirements for the notification timeline. A growing number of vendors now offer emergency notification systems specifically oriented to the campus environment. These campus oriented systems, in most cases, incorporate multiple channels of delivery, including email alerts, automated phone calls, text messages, and in some systems, visual alarms within structures. Emergency notification systems have now, or soon will, become a part of the critical safety infrastructure for most colleges and universities in the United States.

Are the currently available emergency notification systems effective? The apparent rush to adopt such systems post-Virginia Tech may serve to silence the alarm raised by students, faculty, staff and parents, but questions remain as to how effective these systems are in practice. The human factor, both in the generation of alerts, and in the response to them, is critical. Delivery models, to date, focus on multiple channels

J. Löffler and M. Klann (Eds.): Mobile Response, LNCS 5424, pp. 32–40, 2009.
© Springer-Verlag Berlin Heidelberg 2009

and technologies, with institutions typically selecting one or more of these channels for implementation. Can these multiple channels of communication reach all members of the diverse campus population? Students, faculty and staff with disabilities pose key challenges in communicating actionable emergency notifications. Large sub-populations of international students can further pose language barriers in effective communication of emergency information.

In this paper, we focus first on the characteristics of the campus population and the methods used to present emergency notifications. Based upon data collected from initial surveys on one campus, and from publicly available data from surveys conducted on other campuses, challenges to the effectiveness of present systems are discussed. Methods and approaches that can address these challenges are presented.

2 Characteristics of the Campus Population

American colleges and universities range in size from under 1,000 to over 50,000 students. To this population, primarily consisting of young adults in the 18-22 year range, we add faculty and supporting staff. Within the campus population are those who may have one or more disabilities. In a survey of American undergraduates at two and four year institutions, approximately 6% of all students are identified as having a disability [1]. Of these, 29% have a learning disability, 23% have impaired mobility, 16% have a hearing impairment, and 16% have a visual impairment. For a campus similar in size to Rider University (5,700 students), these percentages can translate into approximately 100 students with learning disabilities (such as dyslexia), 55 students who may be unable to hear, and 55 who may have difficulty seeing. In some cases, these disabilities may occur in combination within a single individual. Within the academic context, students (as well as staff and faculty) with disabilities may utilize accommodations in the form of assistive technologies. For those with visual impairments, assistive technologies include screen reading software, screen magnification software and systems, digital talking book players, audio recorders and human note-takers. Those with hearing impairments may use sign language interpreters and captioned multimedia. For these two groups, the disability is mitigated by offering alternative channels or modalities. Those with learning disabilities may utilize a variety of approaches to mitigate the disability, including increased time to complete exams and assignments, reformatting of course materials, and digital talking books which provide synchronized text and audio narration.

International students represent approximately 4% of the total enrollment of US college and university students in 2007 [2], with approximately one third of these students coming from India, China, and Korea. For example, Rider University presently enrolls students from 31 countries. Cultural and language differences may pose significant challenges to these students, particularly during emergencies. For example, signage for basic emergency response, such as fire exits and shelter locations used in the United States typically differs from that used in many other countries. Symbolic signage can ideally transcend language barriers, yet within US campuses, most signage, particularly in relation to exit routes and sheltering remains text based. The campus alerting systems examined utilize text-based messages and support for multiple languages is unclear. A message may be received, but the opportunity for compliance and action is lost if the recipient either does not understand the message or does not recognize the environmental features and cues (e.g., signage) that must be followed in order to comply.

2.1 Technology Utilization in the University Population

Campus emergency notification systems to date are primarily based upon delivery of e-mail, text messages (SMS), and voice calls (reverse 911). Based upon surveys of technology utilization by campus populations, this model of delivery appears justified. As part of the research described in this paper, the authors are conducting a series of online surveys examining the use and experience with the campus emergency notification system by students, faculty, and staff. In the initial survey of Rider University students, 100% of students surveyed reported that they used mobile phones, and 94% had regular access to a personal computer. Though computer usage is limited to "face time" with the system, averaging 4.5 hours per day, 100% of the students report that their mobile phone is on throughout the full day. It should be noted that most initial implementations of emergency notification systems were based upon email alerts. Under that model, students without email capabilities on their phones may not be reachable up to 19.5 hours of the day. Multiple channels of delivery, mobile messages and email, would thus appear to increase the likelihood of receiving a notification.

Mobile phones, given the high adoption rate by university students, thus appear to be the ideal method for delivering emergency notifications. However, actual usage patterns introduce challenges. University undergraduates spend approximately 15 hours in classrooms per week. In our survey, 75% of students report switching their mobile phones into silent mode during class (interestingly, 9.4% report keeping their phones in silent mode throughout the day). The implication of this finding is that during classroom time, students may not immediately detect that an emergency notification has been issued. In practice, however, it is observed that some students will continue to read and respond to text messages during classes, utilizing the vibrate mode of the phone to detect message arrivals. Of the students surveyed, 88.7% report reading text messages immediately when they arrive, though we are continuing to examine actual message reading behavior during classroom time. It can be hypothesized with some confidence that should any individual student receive and read an emergency alert during a class, that information will be shared.

Instant messaging and voice chat applications such as AOL Instant Messenger, MSN Messenger, and Skype have also been proposed as alerting channels, but exhibit the same "face time" challenges of email alerts. A growing number of mobile phones offer access to instant messaging services, leading to the potential of redundant messages to a single device.

The availability of multiple alert formats is one that appears well accepted by students. In our survey of students who signed up for the notification service, multiple modes of message delivery are preferred: 93% selected text messages, 72% selected voice messages, and 68% selected email notifications.

2.2 Participation in Emergency Notification Systems

One of the significant challenges to emergency notification is the opt-in nature of most present systems. In the majority of systems examined, students, faculty, and staff must register to receive the alerts, indicating which mode of message delivery they prefer. At Rider University, 62% of survey respondents reported that they had signed up for the campus emergency notification system. Weiss [3], in a random survey of five US universities, reported participation rates ranging from 31% to 85%.

What limits participation by students? Awareness and motivation appear to be two key factors. Though our analysis is still underway, 38% of the students were either unaware of the emergency notification service or were not sufficiently motivated to undertake the signup process. Are students hindered by the sign up process itself? In the case of Rider, 93% of respondents surveyed who signed up for the service found it easy to do so. On the other hand, the authors have received reports of students with disabilities at a United States mid-west university, specifically those with visual impairments, who found it difficult or impossible to utilize a Web-based sign-up due to the lack of accessibility features in the site design. An analysis of the accessibility of Web-based registration systems is planned by the authors, utilizing the US Section 508 Web Accessibility criteria [4].

To improve participation, schools can elect to make participation mandatory, enforced, for example during registration for academic courses at the start of a school term. This approach can provide for opt-out of the notification system if a student desires to do so.

Other approaches to motivate student participation are being explored, including use of social networking sites and university-supplied intranet student portals to raise awareness. In particular, simple presentation of participation rates by dormitory or year, with a link to the sign up Web site, for example, might serve as one mechanism to motivate students.

3 Technology and Accessibility Issues

Data on actual effectiveness of the notification systems is not clear and vendor claims may paint a rosier picture which may not reflect reality. Statistics can show high rates of message delivery, though action taken as a result of the messages is harder to determine. Of the students in our survey who indicated they had received an emergency notification on their mobile phone, 92% saw the message immediately, but only 51% indicated they took action. It should be noted that only 84% of the students who signed up for emergency notifications reported receiving a notification, raising questions as to whether the sign-up was successfully completed, and if so, whether the system which delivers the notifications actually succeeded in delivering the message to each individual who registered; it may also be possible that the messages simply went unnoticed. Follow-up surveys are seeking to explore this issue in more detail.

3.1 Multimodal Warnings

Multimodal warnings and alerts are advantageous for increasing the likelihood that critical information will be received by the target audience. Vendors of emergency notification systems generally describe their systems as multimodal if they include text messaging, voice calls, electronic displays, and outdoor sirens. Within such multimodal approaches, individuals who have not signed up for a notification service, or who do not have their mobile phone with them may still be alerted by sirens or visual displays. Outdoor sirens, as has been observed in contexts such as tornado or tsunami warning, introduce other problems with respect to eliciting appropriate protective response [5].

For people with sensory disabilities, emergency notification systems may present messages in a form that cannot be detected or understood [6][7]. In order to effectively reach those with sensory disabilities, well designed multimodal alert systems are critical [8][9]. Few vendors make specific mention of accessibility in their systems; those that do present solutions based on the premise that voice calls are accessible to the blind and text messages are accessible to the hearing impaired. Though such an approach may be effective for those two audiences, they do not begin to address the larger scope of accessibility issues encountered with mobile devices themselves, and specific usability issues faced by other disability groups. Individuals with learning and cognitive disabilities may use mobile phones, but may not be able to utilize all features and functions. Complexity of mobile device interfaces is seen as a significant barrier to usage by those with cognitive impairments as well as members of aging populations. Efforts to provide simpler user interfaces can only solve part of the problem; the messages delivered to the phone may be easier to locate, but may present information in a format and style that do not facilitate action.

3.2   Standards for Notifications and Accessibility

Lessons learned from design of accessible information standards can be applied to the design of emergency notification systems. The key approach is to create standard message content with sufficient richness and meta-information to facilitate delivery in multiple modalities, either as an independent channel (voice/audio) or in synchronization with other forms (voice/audio and text). The widespread adoption of the Common Alerting Protocol (CAP) as a standard message format for emergency notifications is a positive step [10]. In practice, and particularly within the context of emergency notifications, CAP usage appears limited to textual presentation with either recorded (natural human) or synthesized speech presentation. To meet the needs of population members who may have learning disabilities, cognitive impairments, or who may not be familiar with the local language, we are particularly interested in adding information to the notification message, primarily in the form of symbolic or graphical images to indicate the nature of the problem and what action to take. Though CAP provides a means to include media types such as images and audio, the approach lacks useful features found in the Synchronized Multimedia Integration Language [11], which forms the basis of accessible information standards like DAISY [12]. SMIL, for example, enables creation of content that includes multiple, parallel channels of information, including multi-lingual content. The model in SMIL is that the system presenting the content, the SMIL player, can apply user and device profiles to choose content tailored to the recipient's device or specific user requirements. A SMIL-based alert message at generation time would include parallel tracks of equivalent information in different modalities, formats, and languages. Though SMIL is supported on some mobile devices, it has not been widely adopted in its present form. The next generation of SMIL, version 3.0 improves upon its modularization model and adds additional support for accessibility, and may yet offer an effective approach for multimodal alerts if wide supported.

Multimedia messaging (MMS) offers one possible current approach to delivering richer information to mobile devices, though at the expense of message size. Though pushing rich media messages out to all members of a campus population poses bandwidth challenges, the fact that small percentages of the overall population may require these messages may not immediately eliminate this approach. Some campus notification systems send email alert messages directly to the mobile phone, which in the case of some mobile devices, are interpreted as MMS message. This "mis-interpretation" in fact adds usability challenges due to the way MMS presents purely text messages on some handsets.

4 Directions for Improved Notification Systems

Can emergency notifications be delivered more effectively, especially for populations who may have difficulties receiving or understanding or responding to the current text-based messaging model? As part of this research, we are exploring notifications and alerts delivered to both mobile devices and to electronic signage within the physical environment. These approaches are discussed in the following sections.

4.1 Mobile Client for Emergency Notifications

As an alternative to pushing rich messages through the network, the authors are exploring a mobile client application that can perform processing on the mobile device itself to transform a standard message that has been received into a richer presentation, tailored to the recipients' needs. Standard symbols, including animations, can be locally stored on the mobile device, and displayed according to the requirements of the notification received. A client application of this nature offers additional capabilities for controlling auditory, tactile, and visual cues based upon the severity of the message received. Design concepts based upon this approach are being explored, and a user interface prototype is in development. Our next step, beginning in the second half of 2008 will be to evaluate the interface concepts with students representing different disability groups using a simulated alert scenario.

Suitability of a format such as CAP, already used in some notification systems, as a source for the transformation is being explored. Figure 1 presents a possible range of information transforms based upon disability type.

One key challenge for the mobile alerting client is an effective model for adoption by the campus community. Mobile device capabilities vary significantly, and it can be expected that not all phones will support application download and execution. Because the primary target of the client application is relatively small, adoption by those with disabilities may be easier to achieve. Several vendors, including one handset manufacturer (Nokia) now offer screen reading features to enable blind and low vision users to effectively interact with their phones. The availability of these phones and their growing adoption of them by the visually impaired, even with the typically higher cost of the device, are promising. Our expectation is that availability of mobile alert clients would be highlighted during the registration process, with instructions for downloading to specific mobile devices provided.

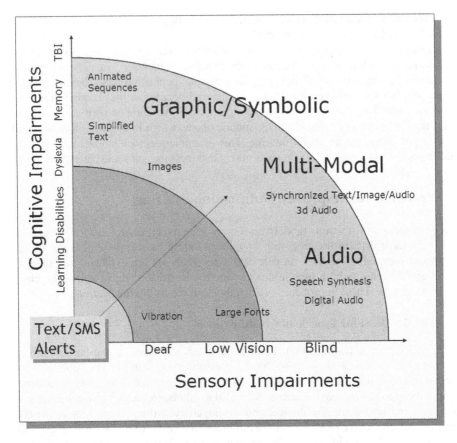

Fig. 1. Presentation Modalities for Alerts based on Disability

4.2 Location-Based Alerts and Dynamic Signage

Location based services, in which the location of the message recipient could be reliably determined offers numerous advantages. In particular, for those with mobility impairments, accessible evacuation routes, location of evac-chairs, or actions (e.g., wait for assistance) will vary. Evacuations or sheltering in place may be determined by one's location on the campus and proximity to the hazard, thus a general message may not be appropriate or easy to interpret. In the case of Rider University, there are actually two campuses, located approximately 6 miles apart. Alerts sent to all students, may in fact only apply to one campus, a problem potentially solved with a location-based approach.

Many campuses now incorporate large flat panel displays in building lobbies and other public areas. Such displays often present building specific or campus wide information and at least one commercial campus notification system provides a means to deliver alert messages as an overlay on the displays. The current text centric approach of campus notification can pose challenges for those with learning and

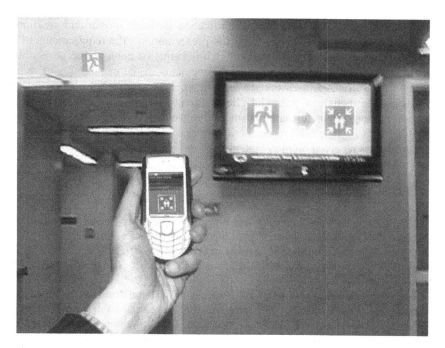

Fig. 2. Symbolic alerts concept, with messages presented on mobile device and digital signage

cognitive impairments, and also for those whose native language may differ from that of the campus population. Figure 2 presents a view of a symbolic alert concept that aligns the mobile alert message with physical signage and electronic displays. Combined with location-based notifications, a recipient of a mobile alert may be informed to evacuate to a shelter area (shown symbolically on the mobile device screen), and dynamic signage within a structure will indicate directional symbols leading to the nearest shelter area, which itself is indicated by a standard shelter sign that appears consistently across the device screen, dynamic signage, and physical signage within the campus environment. Auditory cues, consisting of both spoken instructions and non-speech signals would augment both the mobile and dynamic signage to provide guidance to those with visual impairments.

5 Conclusion

Campus emergency notification systems are coming into widespread use on college and university campuses. The systems in place today are not without problems, ranging from low participation rates to limitations in accessibility for students (and faculty/staff) who may have disabilities and for those who may not be native speakers of the local language. Approaches to improve participation rates include mandatory registration and the use of social networking sites to raise awareness of the system and how to participate in it. Improvements in accessibility are technically more challenging, as it is impacted by the underlying capabilities of the emergency notification system and the delivery devices. Specific approaches to the improving accessibility include enhancement of the emergency notification message format and creation of mobile device applications that can tailor the presentation to the requirements of the device user. Use of standards that support rich information content and accessibility are part of the solution, combined with improvements in the capabilities of mobile devices and the software which is used with them. Two approaches undergoing further investigation include multimodal clients for mobile phones that can transform notification messages into formats that meet the needs of a diverse user community and physical signage that can present notifications and instructions that augment and enhance messages received on mobile devices.

References

1. NCES. Postsecondary Students with Disabilities: Enrollment, services, and persistence. US Department of Education National Center for Education Statistics (June 2000)
2. IIE. Open Doors 2007. Institute of International Education (2007)
3. Weiss, T.R.: A problem IT can't fix: Getting students, faculty to sign up for campus alerts. Computerworld (February 21, 2008)
4. U.S. Government. Section 508 Standards – Subpart B Technical Standards, http://www.section508.gov/index.cfm?FuseAction=Content&ID=12
5. Gregg, C.E., Houghton, B.F., Paton, D., Johnston, D.M., Swanson, D.A., Yanagi, B.S.: Tsunami Warnings: Understanding in Hawai'i. Natural Hazards 40(1), 71–87 (2007)
6. Brooks, M.: Challenges for Warning Populations with Sensory Disabilities. In: Van de Walle, B., Turoff, M. (eds.) Proceedings of the 3rd International ISCRAM Conference, Newark, NJ, USA (May 2006)
7. NCAM. Access to Emergency Alerts for People with Disabilities. WGBH National Center for Accessible Media, http://ncam.wgbh.org/alerts/
8. Hakkinen, M.T.: Human Factors Issues in the Design of Multimodal Public Warning Systems. In: Proceedings of the International Disaster Reduction Conference (IDRC), Harbin, China (August 2007)
9. Hakkinen, M.T., Sullivan, H.T.: Effective Communication of Warnings and Critical Information: Application of Accessible Design Methods to Auditory Warnings. In: Proceedings of Information Systems for Crisis Response and Management Conference (ISCRAM), Delft, Netherlands (May 2007)
10. OASIS. Common Alerting Protocol, v. 1.1, http://www.oasis-open.org/committees/download.php/14759/emergency-CAPv1.1.pdf
11. W3C. Synchronized Multimedia Integration Language (SMIL) 2.1. World Wide Web Consortium (W3C), http://www.w3.org/TR/2005/REC-SMIL2-20051213/
12. DAISY. ANSI-NISO Z39.86-2002. Digital Talking Book Standard. US Library of Congress and The DAISY Consortium, http://www.daisy.org/z3986

Tactical Navigation Support for Firefighters: The LifeNet Ad-Hoc Sensor-Network and Wearable System

Markus Klann

Fraunhofer FIT, Schloss Birlinghoven, 53754 Sankt Augustin, Germany
markus.klann@fit.fraunhofer.de

Abstract. We present a concept and implementation for supporting tactical navigation of firefighters in structural fires, called LifeNet. It is based on a sensor network that firefighters deploy on-the-fly during an intervention and a wearable system that provides them navigational support. The system was designed in collaboration with the Paris Fire Brigade and is based on intensive empirical studies of their work practice. The article focuses on the exploration of human factors related to the LifeNet concept, including appropriation, interaction, as well as the relation to current and potential future work practice. These aspects are discussed for LifeNet and a few related approaches against the findings from our empirical studies.

Keywords: Wearable Computing, Sensor Networks, Firefighting, Navigation, Human-Computer Interaction, Design.

1 Introduction

Since 1993 each year 25 to 35 thousand people reportedly died in fires [1]. In 2003 and 2004, 153 and 198 firefighters died in the line of duty. Additionally, there is substantial economic damage caused by fires. Despite the need to interpret these statistics carefully, they show that fires remain a severe threat to public safety and that firefighting remains a dangerous profession. With the more than 100 annual fatalities among US firefighters in mind and the hope for more resources, an open letter from the year 2000 to then President Clinton states that [2] "*Systems that would enable fire departments to quickly locate downed firefighters are also desperately needed. Why is it America has the technology to track whales across oceans around the world and pinpoint rocks to the centimeter on the surface of Mars, but no devices to accurately pinpoint the location of downed firefighters inside a simple two-story building?*"

This call for systems that allow locating firefighters within building structures addresses an important aspect of the problems described above. In case a firefighter becomes unable to leave an environment that is immediately dangerous to life and health (IDLH) for whatever reason there is a limited timeframe in which the firefighter needs to be located and extracted. There are many examples of accidents during firefighting interventions illustrating that failure to locate firefighters quickly enough or at all is at least a contributing factor to serious injuries or fatalities among firefighters. Hence, systems that effectively support the localization of firefighters

J. Löffler and M. Klann (Eds.): Mobile Response, LNCS 5424, pp. 41–56, 2009.

would indeed increase their safety, as claimed above. Besides increasing safety for firefighters, such systems may also contribute to more effective and efficient fire-fighting operations, increasing chances to extract victims alive or with less severe injuries.

Locating objects or people within buildings has of course been the subject of many research and development efforts. Nonetheless, eight years after the above letter, there is no localization system commercially available that firefighters could use reliably during all relevant interventions. This article argues that the navigational needs of firefighters can be addressed without having to determine their absolute positions and it explores a concept for such a navigational support system, called LifeNet. The key idea of LifeNet is that firefighters moving through a building structure automatically deploy a network of small sensor nodes capable of relative localization among neighboring nodes, exploitable by a wearable system to provide navigation support. This concept is based on intensive empirical studies of work practice with the Paris Fire Brigade and the development is done in close collaboration with them [3]. The concept's principal feasibility has been demonstrated through a physical prototype [4].

The focus of this article is not the concrete underlying technology but the exploration of how this type of navigational support interplays with work practice and of what would be appropriate forms of interaction. The claim of this article is not that the LifeNet concept is a perfect solution to the navigational requirements of firefighters. In fact, there are a number of open questions about the concept and a number of unresolved implementation issues. Instead, this article provides an empirically grounded exploration of the many interesting implications of a particular approach to navigation support, showing how it relates to specific requirements and constraints of the domain, how it fits in with the work practice of firefighters, which principal design options exist, and how and what firefighters may contribute to its development.

In section 2 some related work on indoor localization for firefighters is presented. Section 4 describes the research questions guiding this work. In section 3 relevant aspects of firefighting work practice are explained. Section 5 introduces and discusses the LifeNet concept, followed in section 6 by an overview of a current implementation. In section 7 some results from user studies are presented, including a comparison of two interface variants. In section 8 topics for future work are described.

2 Related Work

There are many different technologies and approaches for locating firefighters: GPS, triangulation with external antennas [5], dead reckoning [6], indoor and outdoor devices, pre-deployed and ad-hoc systems, ultrasound, ultra-wide band, infrared, RFID, radar, RSSI, time of flight, directional antennas, etc. To address the deficits of some of these, hybrid positioning systems have been proposed. Examples include enhancing PDR with a network of ultrasound sensors [7], using fixed RFID tags as waypoints for inertial tracking, using a laser for ad-hoc map creation to support inertial tracking or using minimal map information to support dead reckoning [6]. For the purpose of this article we will concentrate on approaches based on sensor networks.

2.1 Siren

The Siren system is a prototype of a communication system for firefighters directly engaged in structural fires [8]. It consists of PDAs with standard wireless connectivity used by each of these firefighters and sensor nodes (Berkeley motes), one attached to each PDA and others located throughout the structure. The sensor nodes monitor aspects of the environment at their location, including temperature and the presence of close-by firefighters and they can exchange data wirelessly with neighboring nodes. The Siren software running on the PDAs allows for multi-hop messaging between the firefighters tolerant to intermittent connections by way of a store-and-forward mechanism and for a delivery of alerts based on customizable rules depending on contextual parameters obtained through the sensors. To address the operational constraints of firefighters the PDA application is focused on displaying information and affords as explicit interaction only generating a few types of messages by pressing the PDA's keys. The information displayed includes a floor plan with icons showing the status and approximate location of firefighters as well as different kinds of messages. The authors observe that deployment of sensor nodes can either happen before or during an intervention. Firefighters they interviewed pointed out that they would not like to exclusively rely on preinstalled infrastructure and would like tools best that they can operate and maintain themselves. They also suggested that a firefighter could deploy sensor nodes on a dedicated tour of the building as a preparatory step. They authors do not elaborate though how location information such as "room A" gets associated with a given node. While one can imagine that this information gets encoded in preinstalled nodes during their deployment, it is not obvious how this would actually work for an ad-hoc deployment. The authors point out that the communication should be robust to some extent against failing sensor nodes. From their studies of firefighting work practice they conclude that "the fact that a fire hose is always used to allow firefighters to "feel their way out" in case of evacuation reveals that it's very easy to lose orientation in firefighting." Finally, they observe that there are a number of different "points of interaction" within an intervention, including "stairways, fire hoses and the rear of a command vehicle" with different requirements for user interfaces.

2.2 FIRE

Similar to the Siren system, the FIRE project proposes to support firefighters in locating personnel, in communication, in environmental monitoring, and in coordination and control of operations for structural firefighting [e.g. 9]. Similar to Siren, the system consists of a sensor network, called SmokeNet, deployed throughout the building structure, a system with a visual interface for directly engaged firefighters, called FireEye, and a system targeted at incident command outside the building, called eICS. The most noticeable difference probably is that the directly engaged firefighters are not equipped with a PDA but with a wearable computer connected to a micro-display integrated with the breathing mask. The different nodes used for different versions of SmokeNet, for example Telos Sky motes from moteiv, are more recent and powerful but otherwise quite similar to those used for Siren. Another difference is that SmokeNet is composed of different types of nodes, each specializing on particular functions, including an interesting type that is meant to guide occupants during evacuation through visual cues resembling a street light. As for Siren, the underlying assumption is that the SmokeNet is installed within the building prior to the intervention and that digital maps of the building exist that can be shown on the FireEye and eICS systems overlaid with icons for firefighters and other localized entities. In fact, the authors are explicit about targeting large and complex buildings with the apparent rational that the support is particularly needed in these cases and that it is reasonable to assume that fixed SmokeNet installations as well as digital building plans could become available for this class of buildings. As supporting evidence for this rational they point out that SmokeNet could be integrated with other building systems supporting security, energy and usage management, and that there are cities that now require digital plans for buildings beyond a certain height.

Nonetheless, the authors also envision an ad-hoc deployment of SmokeNet. While they do not elaborate on how the positioning is supposed to work for such an ad-hoc deployment, they do explain that the preinstalled sensor network requires calibration in order to attain acceptable positioning quality. Moreover, this quality may still suffer in the form of lag and deviation due to changing environmental conditions such as moving metal doors. The authors may imply the idea that in the ad-hoc case the sensor nodes do not provide localization of firefighters but that they merely support following their trail. While the authors mention that the GUI could offer a simple arrow guiding firefighters to some predetermined location in case they needed to navigate, this is not elaborated and the presented features of FireEye would not support following a trail. The authors offer a few additional suggestions and recommendations relevant for this article. One is that accuracy of information is more important than precision. Another is that the presentation of information must not be suggestive: the user must understand that if the interface shows no dangers this only means that none have been detected, not that none exist. Besides these points more specifically related to the interface and interaction, the authors also raise a number of more general considerations for the design of information technology for firefighters, based on their empirical studies. As the condition of a SmokeNet may degrade over time due to exhaustion of batteries or direct effects of a fire, the network health must be monitored. Also, firefighters strive to reduce their dependency from technologies as much as possible, notably by arranging for fallback procedures. Training is required to enable firefighters to effectively use technologies in highly stressful situations. Finally, as firefighters depend on technologies with their lives, they do not easily trust new technologies and may lose trust easily. The authors comment that the perceived robustness may be very difficult to change by actual robustness and recommend therefore that "Successful implementation of an advanced information technology system for emergency response will require gradual enhancements to the currently used system, and careful consideration of how to gain and maintain trust in the system."

In the light of the numerous challenges in designing new technologies for emergency response, the authors qualify their own research as exploratory. They assert that their system is meant to be complimentary to existing firefighting techniques and requires extensive user testing to determine its actual benefit.

2.3 Dräger's Patent on a Transponder-Based Guidance System

Siren and FIRE are based on pre-deployed networks and only envision a possible ad-hoc deployment without elaborating on how this might work. Somewhat surprisingly, a proposal for this with some noteworthy conceptual differences can be found in a patent initially filed as early as 2004 by Dräger Safety [10]. The core idea of the patent is that a device carried by the user can determine the direction to at least one previously deployed transponder, preferably the nearest, and display information to the user guiding him in that direction. The presented exemplary incarnation of the system is composed of a device mounted below the breathing apparatus of a firefighter, containing a magazine capable of ejecting a number of transponders and being connected to a display that is integrated with the breathing mask and/or helmet. The transponders and the device on the firefighter can communicate information via radio signals such that the device can determine the direction towards the transponder and display this direction to the user. Transponders have IDs uniquely identifying both them and their ejecting device in order to facilitate following the ejection sequence of the transponder trail and correctly navigating through looping or intersecting trails. The transponders are ejected after either i) a certain distance or ii) a certain number of steps or iii) after the signal strength of the last transponder has dropped below a threshold. For option i) the authors assume absolute position information for the transponders to be available through a satellite positioning system, and for option ii) they assume the use of a pedometer. Additionally, an optional "telemetry system" is assumed by the authors to be part of the device for transmitting data between the firefighters inside and outside the building. While in the patent no direct relation is explained between this telemetry system and the guidance system, it is easy to imagine how the former could support the latter, especially because the patent does not mention transmission between the transponders at all. This might not be unrelated to the patent's distinction between active and passive transponders and its careful definition of two variants of the presented algorithm for these two types. The variant for passive transponders addresses their limitations by storing data on the device instead of the transponders. The authors explicitly refer to the passive transponders as RF-ID tags and note that they do not have an independent power supply and can be made light and cheap. By introducing the telemetry system for communication instead of the transponder network the patent avoids having to propose two different solutions for active and passive transponders. The patent names the following specific benefits of the system: i) a user of the device can be guided back along the transponder trail on the path he took while deploying them; ii) a user could be guided on somebody else's transponder trail, for example in the case of a rescue mission; iii) in case absolute positions are available, the length of trail segments can be calculated, for example the length towards an exit or an incapacitated firefighter; iv) the paths and events during travel can be reviewed at a later time. The main observation about this system is that it supports navigation without determining or using absolute positions. As a consequence, it does not support displaying the absolute locations of firefighters, for example on a digital building plan at the command post, as presented by the other projects. The principal technical question that the patent brings up is how the direction to be displayed to the user can be determined by the device and the transponder.

3 Firefighting Work Practice

To ground our work we carried out studies of firefighting work practice with the Paris Fire Brigade (BSPP). These studies started in the autumn of 2004 and are still ongoing as of this writing. They include reviews of the detailed official regulations and intervention reports, formal interviews with several dozen firefighters and informal discussions with many more, as well as observation of demonstrations, several professional trainings and about a dozen large-scale exercises, involving up to several hundred emergency personnel. Moreover, the author himself took part in several days of training in 2005, including how to operate a lifeline during search and rescue operations while using a breathing apparatus, as well as how to operate the water hose during fire attack. Also, in 2006 the author took part in the 3 weeks incident command training, focusing on the upper levels of the chain of command and including theoretical lectures and practical training embedded in large-scale exercises. Our findings are largely consistent and extend the findings reported in [9, 11]. For the purposes of this article, the following will provide a brief account of some relevant aspects of search and rescue operations during firefighting interventions as we have encountered them in our studies.

We assume a scenario with a structural fire in a building of non-trivial complexity where victims are assumed to be located. Standard operating procedures foresee several steps for fighting such a fire, including reconnaissance, extraction of victims and attacking the fire. As the name suggests, reconnaissance is a typically rapid sweep of the operational area to gather information about the type and extent of the fire in order to decide on the next steps. Typically, reconnaissance extends to the border of the area directly affected by the fire which requires proper and more time-consuming fire attack with extinguishing agents. When engaging in these operations, firefighters make use of protective equipment against the fire and tools to help them get in and back out safely, including protective clothing and self-contained breathing apparatuses (SCBA). This equipment affords them a limited protection to operate under these conditions for a certain time, typically well below one hour. Nonetheless, and despite harsh training, several risks remain that may incapacitate an engaged firefighter: i) the environmental conditions may degrade in an unforeseen way, e.g. by a partial structural collapse; ii) the psychological pressure on the firefighter may lead to imprecise perception or judgment, e.g. in a room full of obstacles a firefighter may have difficulties finding back the door through which he entered; iii) tools may simply fail, e.g. a breathing apparatus may be damaged when falling down over some obstacle. Firefighters have adopted operating procedures that, while not being able to eliminate these problems, help in controlling their consequences: a) they always engage in teams of two firefighters staying at arm's length to each other, and retreating immediately when one of them has a problem. This is often called the buddy system; b) the attack teams directly engaging in an IDHL environment operate under the orders and supervision of a team leader who stays in hearing distance at the point of attack immediately outside the IDHL environment and is responsible for a small number of typically not more than 3 attack teams. This team leader receives missions from the command post and reports back to it; c) the team leader has a security team on stand-by to send in after attack teams in need of being rescued. This organization of work introduces considerable redundancy and a certain level of resilience against the failure of tools. Firefighters are equipped with simple horns that they can operate as a distress signal and they have systems that signal an audible alarm in case a firefighter does not move for a certain time or his air tank has reached a critical pressure level.

Due to poor or zero visibility in smoke-filled environments, firefighters make use of ropes, called lifelines, as navigational aids. The two members of an attack team are both attached to one end of a lifeline and the other end gets securely attached at the point of attack outside the IDHL environment. When sweeping their operational area they drag the lifeline behind them, their colleagues at the other end typically holding the lifeline under some tension. The firefighters typically move in a crouched or kneeling position to avoid tripping over obstacles. Eventually, they may decide to attach their end of the lifeline to some object such as a door knob before starting their retreat in order to enable the team replacing them to quickly navigate to their last location. The exploration of an area using lifelines may be a time-consuming gradual process, involving several attack teams. Besides following lifelines established by previous teams to quickly continue their work, firefighters use crayons to put the word "VU" (engl. seen) on doors labeling the rooms they have already searched. Also, attack teams returning from a mission typically scribble simple floor plans as part of their reporting to their team leader and to support the orientation of their colleagues. While team leaders are only responsible for supervising a small number of teams, this task can become surprisingly difficult, given the general pressure of the situation, rotating teams with changing missions, and most importantly vital information such as initial pressure in the air tank as well as time of entry and estimated time of exit for the respective firefighters. To support this supervising task of the team leader, BSPP has introduced in 2006 a technically simple pre-structured portable whiteboard, called reconnaissance management board.

It is probably imaginable to everybody that orientation and navigation in complex building structures with lifelines is not an easy task. Accident reports and also our own observations underline this assumption. Lifelines can get stuck or be cut under doors or other objects, burned by fire, become entangled with furniture, railings etc. and they generally limit the operational range. While firefighters mark the search status of rooms by writing on the doors, these tags can be overlooked, resulting in rooms being searched more than once. Likewise, rooms can also relatively easily be overlooked in complex structures. Alert signals by firefighters are difficult to locate in a noisy fire environment, requiring all the firefighters engaged in the area to retreat in order to account for who is missing. Similarly, acoustic signals used to order firefighters to retreat may not be audible. Another statement we heard repeatedly is that firefighters may get disoriented or incapable of continuing in very small spaces, sometimes even a small single room. While large structures contribute to the difficulties of interventions, small ones can prove to be just as daunting. For the question of navigational support, it is important to know that firefighters may not be able to sweep the entire operational area during an initial reconnaissance because parts of the area directly affected by the fire may require proper fire attack using the water hose. For this article, the single most important result from our studies is that traditional lifelines afford a navigational support tool without providing localization.

4 Research Questions

Our research was partly inspired by the promising possibilities of sensor networks. We thought of them not so much as a matured technology that could readily be applied to this domain but more as a relatively young visionary technological concept. We were aware that there were still many difficult technological problems to resolve, such as making sensor nodes that tolerate rough physical handling. We were also aware that many trade-offs exist between desired system properties, such as between size, weight, autonomy, price, communication range and positioning accuracy. We assumed that there was probably not a single optimal combination of these properties, but a number of suitable combinations with respective advantageous and disadvantages. Our interest was in exploring this design space of possible options and not primarily in resolving technological problems. Our perspective on this task is that the advantageous and disadvantages of any specific design have to be judged on the basis of a thorough assessment of the supported work practice. From our studies we knew about a number of constraints and requirements of firefighting work practice and we wanted to investigate how a possible solution would need to address them.

Probably the most salient assumption underlying this design exploration is that firefighters do not strictly require a system that enables identifying the absolute position of a firefighter within a structure but rather a system that supports them reliably in following previously established paths such as when sending a rescue team to extract an incapacitated colleague or when starting their own retreat. Moreover, the lifeline is a trusted tool that is used successfully in many interventions although it also has a number of deficiencies that have let to sometimes fatal accidents in the past. Therefore we were interested in studying how sensor networks could be used to provide a similar kind of navigational support while at the same time avoiding as many of the deficiencies as possible. Additionally, we were interested in how firefighters would appreciate and could make optimal use of such a new support system, given its largely different properties and our observation that the relatively safe and efficient use of established tools is achieved by embedding them in a work practice developed and proven through extended experience. Related questions then are who should actually receive what information to ensure safe and efficient operations, how can sensor networks be made at least as reliable as traditional lifelines, and – quite a different question – how can the perceived reliability of the system be made to correspond well with its actual reliability and inspire an appropriate amount of trust with its users.

The second assumption underlying this design exploration is that the system would have to work without a preinstalled infrastructure and without maps. From our experience, neither one nor the other is available for the vast majority of buildings and this is not likely to change substantially for many years. And in case they are available, firefighters will still want a backup solution. The resulting questions are how the ad-hoc deployment of the sensor network can be achieved and how the navigational requirements of firefighters can be met without maps. Related questions are what kind of update frequency, precision, accuracy and deployment density is needed to enable a sufficient navigation support. These questions are tightly connected to work practice in that firefighters have trained skills in navigating environments with poor visibility and a support system needs only to provide enough support to successfully complement these skills. Another aspect of system design is that partial failure should only degrade the system gradually and gracefully.

Generally, regarding the interaction with the system, firefighters consistently ask for extreme simplicity given the physical and psychological demands of their primary activities. On the other hand there are situations in which more complex interactions seem possible and helpful. The question here is where to find the right balance and also whether different conditions can benefit from different forms of interaction.

5 The LifeNet Concept – Overview and Discussion

With LifeNet we refer to a system for supporting firefighters during search and rescue missions in structural fires. From the start of our design we used scenarios as a way of describing current work practice and envisioning how the work could look like in the future, assuming the availability of certain technologies. Similar to [11], we found that scenarios were helpful in focusing on user requirements and expressing technological concepts in a generally understandable form. In our experience, scenarios were also well suited for engaging firefighters in participating in their creation [12].

In autumn 2004 we created a set of 10 scenarios, drawing on literature studies of firefighting work practice and on two workshops with BSPP dedicated to scenario-writing and validation. In particular, we learned about the current work practice during search and rescue operations in structural fires as described in section 3. Without being aware at the time of the sensor network based systems presented in section 2, we were inspired by the idea of using distributed sensor networks. So we created vision scenarios on how this work could be supported with a wearable system for the engaged firefighters and an ad-hoc deployed sensor network, including:

Eletronic Lifeline: *An attack team enters a complex building structure. Each fireman carries a considerable quantity of small, light and robust devices called lifeline beacons. Each lifeline beacon sends out a signal that each fireman can use to determine his orientation and his distance from this beacon. The signal has a certain range and whenever a fireman moves away from any of the beacons more than a certain distance he is alerted to place the next beacon. As the firemen enter the building they place the lifeline beacons whenever needed, for example at corridor junctions. The signal of the lifeline beacons would contain information on who placed the beacon and at what time. After being deployed the lifeline beacons collect information on the temperature and the air quality around them and also on whether they have been moved. This way each fireman creates an electronic lifeline that can guide his way back out of the building. The firemen can perceive the lifeline in different ways, depending on how much other information is available. When there is no other information available the firemen can hear an acoustic signal that indicates the direction and distance to the next beacon or a similar graphical representation on their displays. If there is additional information available, such as an electronic building map, the whole lifeline may be represented as dots on this map. The environmental data collected by the lifeline beacons is used to create a more precise representation of the conditions at the respective location. Additionally, the lifeline beacons could also receive information from the firemen and from their neighbouring beacons. This way, each beacon could collect information about his neighbourhood such as the firemen that are or have been in the vicinity and other beacons that have been placed around it. One advantage of this is that the beacons can provide valuable additional information to other firemen that are close by (especially for search and rescue). The other big advantage is that information from one beacon can move to the next beacon and this way information can get out of the building to the command post even if there is* *no communication network that covers the whole area. This way, the command post gradually can build up a better understanding of the situation and progress inside the building. And in the case that several firemen have searched the building systematically there is not only one lifeline but actually a lifenet of beacons. This is extremely important to guide firemen out of the building that cannot take the same path anymore which they had used for entering the building because, for example, the floor has collapsed.*

Search with Life Beacons: *A team of firemen has arrived at the smoke-filled 5th floor of a burning apartment building to search for people that are expected to be trapped there. They engage in searching the rooms following the standard procedures. But instead of putting their lamp at the entrance to signal to other firemen that they are currently searching this room and instead of putting chalk marks on the door to indicate whether this room has already been searched they use "electronic life beacons" for this purpose. Whenever they enter a room the team leader puts down a life beacon. Through a simple voice command he puts the life beacon in "search" status, indicating to other firemen in the vicinity and to the command post that this room is currently being searched. Before leaving the room he gives another voice command which puts the life beacon in "searched" mode indicating that this room has already been searched. The life beacons' status is clearly displayed to other firemen through different symbols on their visors or different acoustic signals. Shortly after entering the next room the search team discovers an unconscious person on the floor. They communicate with the command post which decides that they can send in a rescue team fast enough to retrieve the victim and that the search team should continue because other people are likely to be found in the other rooms. The search team places a life beacon on the victim and through voice-control puts it into "victim" mode to ensure that the rescue team will find its way.*

After the creation of these initial scenarios we continued with empirical studies of search and rescue work practice during training exercises as explained in section 3. Through these studies we acquired a more in-depth understanding of the collaborative, dynamic and spatial aspects of these operations, confirming some of the assumptions and ideas included in the scenarios and suggesting some possible modifications.

Our studies confirmed that being able to tag locations with tactically relevant information such as search status of rooms or located victims could help in avoiding omissions or duplications. They also confirmed that communication across the LifeNet could help in mitigating the limitations of today's radio communication for monitoring and time-critical alerting. They appreciated the idea of using beacons deployed by other teams for additional navigation options, although they asked how the system could safely guide the firefighters in switching from one beacon trail to another. Some questions were raised though on how engaged firefighters would interact with the system. In particular, firefighters were skeptical about voice input and output due to the noisy environment and possible interference with radio communication.

A central question we were asking in these studies was whether an absolute positioning system was required, enabling to locate firefighters on a map if available, or whether navigational support along the beacon trails was sufficient, based on positioning of firefighters relative to neighboring beacons only. We considered this question to be of particular importance because of its implications not only for the functionality provided to the firefighters but also because of the different requirements for implementing the respective system. While a map representation was clearly appreciated by firefighters, they said that a navigational support system that would allow them to effectively follow the beacon trails while being clearly superior to the standard lifeline would also be a very helpful tool. From a technical point of view, such a relative positioning system seemed considerably more feasible and also left the option open to use a simpler and cheaper interface than a high-resolution micro-display.

In our field studies though we also learned the important lesson that firefighters would not easily give up their accustomed lifeline for a sensor network. Besides being generally reluctant to drop a well-known and proven tool, they were also skeptical about the durability of the sensor nodes and the dependency from the wearable system. Moreover, the physical quality of the lifeline, literally tying the two buddies of an attack team to the firefighter supervising them at the entry point, apparently is a psychologically important factor making it very difficult to trust a system without this quality. In our concept, we decided to address this issue by envisioning the two obvious options: 1) integrating the beacons into the lifeline; 2) including features in the system with the potential to compensate the absence of the physical lifeline. To this end, firefighters suggested or confirmed to e.g. put flashing lights on the beacons to provide a fallback visual navigation aid in case the rest of the system fails, as well as including appropriate feedback about beacon ejection, remaining beacons and the state of the connection to their buddy and supervisor. We also learned that automatic deployment of beacons was preferred due to the physical and cognitive demands of SaR operations, with the possibility of simple manual deployment as a fallback. When thinking about a deployment concept we realized that there were several factors to consider: i) the building structure; ii) the movement of firefighters; iii) the operation of the sensor network; iv) tactical considerations by the firefighters. In particular, the related points i) and ii) could be addressed by using a motion sensor on the firefighter that may not only count steps but also detect changes in direction which is important information for retracing paths accurately.

The question of guiding firefighters along the same paths taken while deploying the beacons is important. While conditions can change rapidly and dramatically during firefighting interventions, it is reasonable to exploit the information present in a path once travelled successfully, provided that the firefighters retracing a path apply an appropriate level of prudence just like the ones who originally established it. This insight is arguably the core of the concept. The system does not try to provide general absolute positioning but an enhanced navigational aid that makes use of and supports the existing navigational skills and senses of firefighters.

Another essential finding was that the firefighter at the point of attack should be the recipient of information about the team members he is supervising, and not the command post. Similarly, directly engaged firefighters should be presented with as little information as possible to avoid overload but also not to stimulate anxiety about their current condition, possibly resulting in a constant unnecessary and distracting monitoring of their own heart-rate etc. Instead, this monitoring should be done by their supervisor. Regarding the system to be used by the supervising firefighter, it would be desirable to be able to share information with his team members because before engagement, they discuss and agree on tactics. While this shows that an adapted distribution of information and functions over several systems was desirable, we also realized that in case connection to levels higher up in the hierarchy was lost, systems at lower levels needed to be able to provide sufficient information to enable their users to take safe and effective actions independently.

6 Implementing LifeNet

To focus on the conceptual aspects of LifeNet and avoid the many technical challenges of implementing a functional physical system, we started exploring possible implementations of the LifeNet concept by developing and using a multi-player virtual environment for simulating firefighting interventions, called FireSim. Currently, this implementation allows testing many functions of LifeNet, including automatic on-the-fly deployment of beacons, navigation support to selected beacons and the visual interface for the users.

In parallel we started implementing a physical implementation of the LifeNet system. The wearable part of this system was done in the wearIT@work project and for the sensor network part we collaborated with another EU research project focusing on relative positioning with sensors, called Relate. The essential elements of our current physical LifeNet implementation are shown in Fig. 1. As in the FIRE system, we

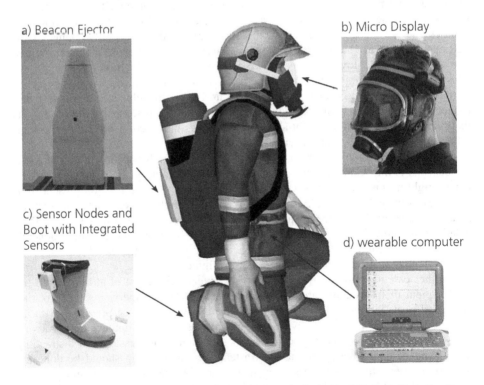

a) Beacon Ejector

b) Micro Display

c) Sensor Nodes and Boot with Integrated Sensors

d) wearable computer

Fig. 1. The LifeNet system: A wearable computer (d) controls the deployment of beacons from the ejector (a), receives positioning information from the beacons integrated with the boots (c) and presents navigational information on a micro-display integrated in the breathing mask (b)

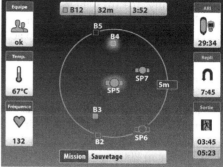

Fig. 2. Two variants of the LifeNet interface for the micro-display: Variant 1, left) the direction towards the next beacon (B4) is indicated by an arrow and the distance by a bar. Variant 2, right) Detected objects within a certain range, including the next beacon to navigate to are displayed as icons around the firefighter in the centre.

decided to use a micro-display integrated within the breathing mask. This display shows the visual interface to the firefighter. The interface does not present a map. Instead it shows an egocentric representation of the user's vicinity (Fig. 2). In variant 2, the user is represented by an icon in the middle and detected objects within a certain range, including beacons and other firefighters, are represented by icons within the circle. In particular, the beacon the firefighter is currently supposed to navigate to is represented by a special beacon icon. Objects that can still be detected but are outside the range are represented by different icons on the circle. The field at the bottom of the interface gives the current mission which is "rescue" in this case. If the current mission involves navigating to a known beacon, the field at the top indicates the ID of this beacon as well as the estimated distance and time to reach it. From top to bottom, the fields on the left of the interface indicate whether the connection to the user's buddy is ok, the current surrounding temperature and the current heart-rate. The fields on the right indicate the remaining breathing time, the time until the firefighter has to start his retreat, and the times to the nearest and second-nearest exit, if available. In other words, this interface requires as input the relative location of objects in the vicinity and provides navigational support on this basis.

The LifeNet beacons are implemented using custom-made sensor nodes from the Relate project, also known as bricks. Their main characteristic regarding LifeNet is that two bricks can determine the distance and angle between them. To this end each brick has a radio module and ultrasound transducers on each of its four sides. As shown in Fig. 1, both boots of the firefighter were fitted with a brick, the main unit being attached to the top of the shaft and the four transducers being attached to the four sides of the shoe right above its sole. More details on this can be found in [4].

A considerable constraint of the current beacon implementation is that they are not robust enough to be dropped on the ground and that they are two big for a useful number to be stored in a beacon ejector of reasonable size. We addressed this problem in two ways. First, we designed dummy beacons suitable for ejection and a corresponding ejector based on our assumptions of how small specialized sensors could be made for this application. Second, for user tests we pre-deployed bricks in a realistic pattern. Finally, the firefighter uses a computing unit that has a wired connection to the micro-display for rendering the visual interface, and a wireless connection to the two bricks integrated with the boots to acquire the sensor data for processing.

7 User Studies

We have implemented LifeNet both as a physical and a virtual prototype, each focusing on different aspects and each with a specific set of supported functionality. In the following we report on one user study for each implementation.

At UbiComp 2007 we made a demonstration of the physical LifeNet implementation with the Relate bricks [4]. We had pre-deployed a dozen or so beacons in a curvy Y-shaped layout. We asked visitors to put on the wearable system and try to follow one branch of the Y-path to the tip and return on the other branch. Due to the processing capabilities at the time, we had to use a very simple interface, consisting of an arrow indicating the direction and a bar indicating the distance to the next beacon on the current trail. The visitors who tried the system were able to follow the path with more or less difficulty. The main problem was that the calculation of the relative position between the beacons on the ground and the beacons on the user took up to a few seconds, creating a considerable lag in the display of the navigation interface which led to some level of disorientation at times. Therefore, while the demonstration showed the feasibility of navigational support based on the LifeNet approach, it also revealed that the limitations of this implementation were too severe to allow for a satisfactory navigational experience for the users.

In June 2007, we conducted a user study of the virtual LifeNet implementation at BSPP headquarters. In particular, we studied different interface variants for the wearable system. The environment represented the BSPP training house. Four firefighters could take part in the simulation simultaneously, steering their respective virtual firefighters through the building, deploying LifeNet beacons and observing information on their virtual micro-displays that were shown as part of the first-person view. The simulation represented smoke by virtual fog, effectively impairing vision such that only close-by objects were discernible. We used this to ask firefighters within the building to find their way back by following the indications on their micro-display. In this study we were interested in learning which of two interface variants we had defined would be favored by the firefighters. The variants are shown in Fig. 2. We had two groups of about 6 firefighters each for two consecutive simulation sessions (with some fluctuation of people). Before the simulation runs we asked firefighters which interface variant they would prefer. About half of the participants said they would prefer variant 1 because of its simplicity. After experiencing the interfaces during the simulation runs, all participants stated that they would prefer variant 2. Some participants pointed out that variant 2 had the advantage of providing a better understanding of the immediate environment. Generally, the participants stated that while the navigational information seemed adequate, information about temperature, health and time indications should be less detailed and should be presented with as little text as possible to increase readability.

8 Future Work

The most important and imminent step in our future research is investigating the LifeNet usage during trial interventions at the BSPP training house. Due to the limitations of our current physical implementation of LifeNet mentioned in section 6, we will simulate part of its functionality by a combination of our virtual simulation and Wizard of Oz techniques [13]. We will also explore the integration of beacons with the traditional lifeline as well as other implementations for beacons such as with RFID tags. Regarding work practice we will address e.g. monitoring and maintaining network health over the lifetime of an intervention as well as integration with scribbling building maps.

Acknowledgments. The presented research is supported by the European Commission as part of the wearIT@work project (contract no. 004216). I'd like to thank the participants of the Relate project (contract no. 013790) for the collaboration in creating a physical implementation of the LifeNet system. Also, I'd like to thank my colleague Patrick Klein from BIBA for his collaboration in creating the physical beacon ejector and dummy beacons, the participants from Carl Zeiss for integrating one of their micro-displays into the breathing mask, and my colleague Lars Zahl from Fraunhofer FIT for his help in improving the visual appearance of my LifeNet interface design. My special thanks go to the Paris Fire Brigade for their participation as end-users and their valuable feedback and support.

References

1. Brushlinsky, N.N., et al.: Fire Statistics - Report No. 11, International Association of Fire and Rescue Services, CTIF (2006)
2. NEEDA. Draft Letter to President Clinton in Support of Fire Bill in US Congress (2000) [cited 09/17/2008],
   http://www.needa.org/PublicNewsletter.cfm?ID=543
3. Klann, M.: Playing with Fire: User-Centered Design of Wearable Computing for Emergency Response. In: CHI Extended Abstracts (2007)
4. Klann, M., et al.: LifeNet: an Ad-hoc Sensor Network and Wearable System to Provide Firefighters with Navigation Support. In: UbiComp: Demos Extended Abstracts, Innsbruck, Austria (2007)
5. NSF, SBIR Phase II: Wireless Firefighters Lifeline, in Matchmaker programm technology prospectus FY 2000-2007, p. 449 (2008)
6. Beauregard, S., Klepal, M., Widyawan: Indoor PDR Performance Enhancement using Minimal Map Information and Particle Filters. In: IEEE/ION Position, Location and Navigation Symposium (PLANS) (2008)
7. Fischer, C., et al.: Ultrasound-aided pedestrian dead reckoning for indoor navigation. In: 1st ACM international workshop on Mobile entity localization and tracking in GPS-less environments, pp. 31–36. ACM, New York (2008)
8. Jiang, X., et al.: Siren: Context-aware computing for firefighting. In: Ferscha, A., Mattern, F. (eds.) PERVASIVE 2004. LNCS, vol. 3001, pp. 87–105. Springer, Heidelberg (2004)
9. Wilson, J., et al.: A Wireless Sensor Network and Incident Command Interface for Urban Firefighting. In: MobiQuitous 2007 (2007)

10. Meyer, J.-u., et al.: Device and process for guiding a person along a path traveled, Dräger Safety AG&Co. KGaA (DE), US Patent No. 7209036 (2007)
11. Baber, C., Haniff, D.J., Woolley, S.I.: Contrasting paradigms for the development of wearable computers. IBM Systems Journal: Issue on Pervasive Computing 38(4), 551–565 (1999)
12. Klann, M.: Playing with Fire: User-Centered Design of Wearable Computing for Emergency Response. In: Löffler, J., Klann, M. (eds.) Mobile Response 2007. LNCS, vol. 4458, pp. 116–125. Springer, Heidelberg (2007)
13. Yang, L., Jason, I.H., James, A.L.: Topiary: a tool for prototyping location-enhanced applications. In: ACM UIST (2004)

Improving the Communication of Spatial Information in Crisis Response by Combining Paper Maps and Mobile Devices

Johannes Schöning[1,2], Michael Rohs[2], Antonio Krüger[1], and Christoph Stasch[1]

[1] Institute for Geoinformatics, University of Münster,
Robert-Koch-Str. 26-28, 48149 Münster, Germany
[2] Deutsche Telekom Laboratories, TU Berlin,
Ernst-Reuter-Platz 7, 10587 Berlin, Germany

Abstract. Efficient and effective communication between mobile units and the central emergency operation center is a key factor to respond successfully to the challenges of emergency management. Nowadays, the only ubiquitously available modality is a voice channel through mobile phones or radio transceivers. This makes it often very difficult to convey exact geographic locations and can lead to misconceptions with severe consequences, such as a fire brigade heading to the right street address in the wrong city. In this paper we describe a handheld augmented reality approach to support the communication of spatial information in a crisis response scenario. The approach combines mobile camera devices with paper maps to ensure a quick and reliable exchange of spatial information.

1 Introduction and Motivation

Recently a misconception of a location led a German fire brigade to a wrong place (as noted in the abstract the fire brigade headed to the right street address, but in the wrong city) in this case with terrible consequences [1]. The webpage [2] gives a very similar example of an ambulance that was sent to a wrong address. However, information on locations is not only important when talking about street addresses, but also when mobile units need to enter hazardous areas, such as a flooded area or a forest fire. In such situations graphics and maps are needed in addition to verbal communication between the mobile unit and the control center in order to ensure that the right action is performed in the right location.

Currently paper-based maps are used in conjunction with the voice channel (either through phones or radio transceivers) to achieve agreement on locations between mobile units and the control center. Computer-based displays (as provided in tablet PCs, PDAs and mobile phones) are infrequently used, because they are too small and of too low resolution to handle this task successfully. Larger displays are too heavy or not ruggedized enough to suit the task. Even in the advent of electronic paper [3], one cannot expect robust large-scale electronic maps in the near and midterm future.

J. Löffler and M. Klann (Eds.): Mobile Response, LNCS 5424, pp. 57–65, 2009.
© Springer-Verlag Berlin Heidelberg 2009

For these reasons we propose an approach where smaller mobile devices (which can easily be ruggedized) are combined with conventional large scale laminated paper maps of the environment. In particular, we argue that if a modern camera-equipped mobile phone is used, information about locations can be easily conveyed by using the available voice channel and a mobile augmented-reality approach. In this approach a mobile device is moved like a *magic lens* [4] over a printed map and location information is superimposed onto the map in real time. Our hypothesis is that with this additional modality communication errors are heavily reduced in comparison to the voice channel alone. Large scale maps can provide an excellent overview of the whole situation, which would not be possible with the device screen alone.

The integrated cameras can also be used to quickly capture up-to-date photographs of the situation on the spot. These documents can then be linked to positions on the map as multimedia annotations created by the mobile units. Relying on our earlier work on mobile camera phone interaction with paper maps [5] we have developed multi-modal interaction concepts suited to the emergency tasks at hand, which are presented in the remainder of the paper.

The paper is organized as follows. In Section 2 we briefly describe a scenario which underlines the significance of our approach. We discuss related work in Section 3 and introduce the multimodal interaction concepts in Section 4. Section 5 reports the current state of the implementation and a conclusion and summary is provided in Section 6.

2   Scenario

In our hypothetical scenario, floodwaters strike the eastern part of Germany, eventually causing a flood that affects villages and cities, for example the historic downtown of Dresden, along the river Elbe. Evacuation alerts are sent out to the affected populated areas. The Technisches Hilfswerk (THW)[1] constantly inspect all banks and dams to ensure that leaky parts are detected early. On an inspection walkway a THW team gets a call from the Emergency Operation Centre (EOC): A helicopter has reported a leaky spot in the bank on a specific position P with the geographic coordinates (X, Y). The bank is about to break and a THW team has to prevent this by sealing it with sandbags. In this case it is necessary to communicate the exact position P from the EOC to the mobile unit to be sure not to waste valuable time. Of course, this communication channel is not unidirectional. There are situations in which this communication is needed in the other direction as well. Let us assume, for example, that the THW team has detected a leaky spot and needs more sandbags and more manpower to protect the bank. Describing the position verbally or exchanging the coordinates of a position P literally as X and Y via the voice channel is a time consuming and error-prone task [6]. We illustrate this problem in Figure 1.

---

[1] The Technisches Hilfswerk (THW) is the governmental disaster relief organization of the Federal Republic of Germany.

Fig. 1. Problem of exchanging spatial information via the voice channel

The way dynamic geo features, such as the approaching floodwater, are visualized on the map obviously has a strong effect on the usefulness and understandability of the presented location information. This can be easily done in the EOC by using large dynamic map displays, but it is challenging task to realize a dynamic map application for THW teams in the field. Tablet PCs still are unhandy and have a short battery runtime. PDAs and smartphones with network connectivity can provide dynamic maps with the desired content by querying an adequate web service, but these maps suffer from the small display size. Because visual context is lacking, it is often hard to identify locations and landmarks on these maps, rendering them rather useless.

3   Related Work

Collaborative visualization and decision-making tools for crisis response have been classical fields of the Digital Cartography, Visualization and GIS communities. In addition, other disciplines, such as the HCI and Ubiquitous Computing communities, have tried to tackle various aspects of this problem. Most of the existing work focuses on large format map applications that support decision-making, for example, in an emergency operation center (EOC). McEachren [7] et al. provide a good overview of these large format map applications that support collaborative visualization and decision-making. The GIS wallboard [8] is a conceptual example of an electronic white board envisioned to support sketch-based gestures to interact with geospatial data. Other systems, designed especially for tablet PCs were implemented by Oviatt [9] and Egenhofer [10]. Sharma et al. [11] concentrate on multi-modal interaction (speech and gesture) with a large dynamic map display and evaluated that system in a crisis response scenario with real users. All this work concentrates on supporting decision-making and group collaboration in an EOC, but does not concentrate on the problem of the communication between mobile units and the EOC. We provide an easy, intuitive and robust system trying to tackle that problem.

In the HCI community Palen and Liu [12] describe new perspectives on citizen-based activities that arise out of peer-to-peer communications in disaster activities. These activities serves important tactical, community-building, and emotional functions. Since our approach does not require special-purpose hardware it could also be used by the general public to be informed and to provide feedback and take part in the crisis response activities. Yuan et al. [13] propose a concept for an intelligent mobile crisis response system (CRS) that would have facilitated a more effective response in a given scenario. They list six critical tasks of a CRS (Monitoring and Reporting, Identification, Notification, Organization, Operation, Assessment and Investigation) and outline several solutions to improve theses tasks.

In this paper we describe a concrete application of a communication system between mobile units and an EOC trying to support communication of spatial information between them, as well as other critical tasks in a CRS like *Monitoring and Reporting* and *Identification and Notification* [13]. This work differs from the related work in that we apply a combination of two devices typically used by mobile units, namely mobile camera phones and paper maps. Combining both we can provide a robust and intuitive way to easily support the communication of any kind of spatial information.

4   Basic Interaction Concept

As described before, the communication between the EOC and the units in the field typically happens via the voice channel today. This modality makes the rapid and accurate communication of spatial information difficult. In our approach the voice channel is augmented by visual information that is presented on the mobile device screen (see Figure 2). Since the device screen is too small to help the user to easily acquire overview knowledge for a spatially extended area, we combine the handheld display with a medium to large size laminated paper map (A5 to A2 size). The paper map provides the static long-term information of the area, which is not affected by the crisis event, such as landscape features or street names. The paper map can still be updated regularly. Since (even laminated) paper is cheap, a new map could be handed out once a day, which includes recent changes induced by the crisis (see Figure 3). The paper map is easily transportable, robust, does not require any power supply, and in effect constitutes a high-resolution display.

The mobile device with an integrated camera is used as a *magic lens* [4] for the paper map. It analyzes the part of the paper map that is visible in the camera view and determines the current focus position on the map. The device shows dynamic overlay graphics and textual information that reflect the most up-to-date state of the crisis. As the situation changes or as new requirements and tasks are communicated by the EOC, the map is updated in real time. During a phone conversation, virtual annotations of map areas can be created in the EOC

Fig. 2. Supporting the exchange of spatial information by combining the voice channel and the visualization on the mobile device

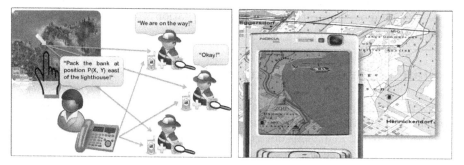

Fig. 3. 1:n Communication between the control center and the first responder (left). Showing an augmented (or alternative) view of the printed map (right).

and the result becomes immediately visible on the display of the first responder (or vice versa). This concept achieves maximum transfer of spatial information at minimum reliance on special-purpose technology and is therefore expected to be quite robust. The camera phone as well as the paper (or cardboard) map can easily be ruggedized. By combining the voice channel and the visual channel, tasks and needs can effectively and unambiguously be communicated.

4.1 1:1 Communication between the Control Center and the First Responder

Figure 2 illustrates one-to-one communication between the control center and the team member. Figure 2, left, is an example of communication from the EOC to the THW team. The EOC issues a command to the leader of a THW team that involves a spatial target to operate on—in this case a bank that needs to be protected. Figure 2 (right) shows, how a specific requirement, again involving a spatial component, is communicated from the first responder to the EOC. In both cases the involved location can be accurately determined by the first responder, when using the *magic lens* approach.

4.2   1:n Communication between the Control Center and the First Responder

Normally, a single task is collaboratively performed by a large number of THW teams in the field. The EOC has to issue out the task to the group as quickly as possible. Again, the *magic lens* approach enables the team members to individually receive voice commands and review the graphical annotations of the map using their personal displays. Even a single large paper map can be collaboratively shared by multiple THW team members by using multiple camera phones.

This one-to-many communication is not limited to the EOC. One team member might need to quickly send information about a spatial object to the others nearby. In this case he or she would create a graphical annotation or select an icon from a library of icons, place it at the intended location, and attach a textual or voice annotation to this icon. This annotation would then be visible to the other first responders in the vicinity.

5   State of Implementation and Usability Test

Figure 4 shows the prototype architecture. The mobile device is tracked over the map using the algorithm described in [14], which relies on a tiny dot grid that is printed on the paper map. This dot grid allows pixel precise augmentation of the paper map on the mobile device screen in a robust way (see Figure 3 left). Given the different test maps with about 500 patches, the current implementation (with 12×12 samples per patch) processes 8 to 12 frames per second on a Nokia N95, depending on the number of patches found in the camera frame. The map can be rumbled to a certain degree without severely affecting the recognition rate.

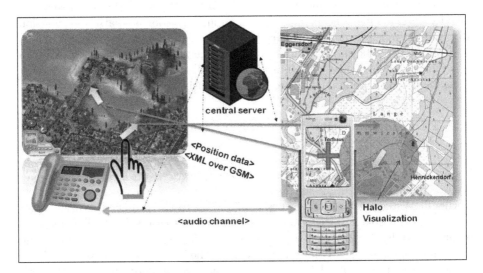

Fig. 4. System architecture of the application

The spotlight integrated next to the camera lens on many camera phones can be used to illuminate the map in low light conditions.

The voice channel is established via a normal phone call (see Figure 4, green arrow, labeled *voice channel*). Spatial information displayed on the large map display, like the actual flood water level, in the EOC can be easily transferred via a specific XML protocol using GSM or, if available, via UMTS. (see Figure 4, red arrows, labeled *position data*).

The question of the relative benefit of this interaction technique compared to two other navigation techniques that only use the mobile device display for map visualization was already presented in [15]. In a formal user study the performance of three methods for map navigation with mobile devices was compared. These methods were joystick navigation, the dynamic peephole method without visual context, and the magic lens paradigm, as described in this paper, using external visual context like paper maps. We measured user performance and motion patterns and collected subjective preference via questionnaires. The results demonstrate the advantage of dynamic peephole and magic lens interaction over joystick interaction in terms of search time and degree of exploration of the search space.

Additionally we casually observed different visual exploration strategies. Some subjects constantly focused on the mobile display to find the next target, others switched their gaze to the background map to identify a target region, moved their mobile to that area and finally fixated the display again.

Off-screen information can be visualized with the *Halo* technique [16] or the *Wedge* technique [17]. The former draws a ring around off-screen objects that reaches into the border of the device display. From the position and curvature of the ring segment the user can infer the approximate direction and distance of the off-screen object. The Wedge technique increases scalability by drawing "pie Wedges" instead of circles and lays them out such that overlap is avoided if possible. In user studies it was found that both techniques provided equally good cues about the distance of the off-screen object. To illustrate the basic

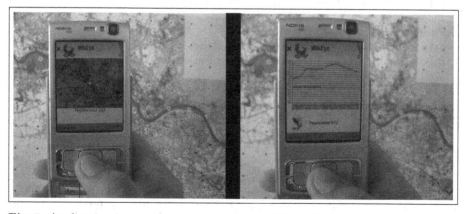

Fig. 5. Application in use. A user is acquiring additional information about a water level sensor using the mobile phone like a magic lens over a paper map.

principle of operation, a video of a mobile magic lens for paper maps is available under http://www.youtube.com/watch?v=5Z_D5JNcfuQ and the figure 5 shows the application in an emergency scenario. It shows the Wikeye [18] application, in which geo-referenced Wikipedia content is made accessible by moving a camera phone over the map. The live camera image of the map is enhanced by graphical overlays of the hyperlinked objects and snippets of Wikipedia content.

6   Conclusion and Future Work

We described a method to support the communication of spatial information in crisis response situations. The method combines standard mobile camera devices with printed maps to ensure a quick and reliable exchange of spatial information. We use a robust mobile augmented reality tracking approach to generate overlay graphics at interactive rates. The tracking technique has been successfully deployed in a number of applications [5], [18], [19], [20] and [21] . However, this work is at an early stage and we mainly presented concepts and ideas that have to be verified in usability tests and in training exercises in the field. The infrastructure that allows for communication between the EOC and the team is under development. Nonetheless, we are convinced of the applicability and practical value of the proposed concepts and look forward to take this work further. In terms of usability tests we particularly want to focus on users under stress with little time and little attention available for mobile map interaction. As a next step we plan to conduct a structured interview with a manager of the EOC of the Berlin fire brigade to give a first impression of the feasibility and acceptability of such an application.

References

1. WDR online (German only) (2008),
   http://www.wdr.de/themen/panorama/brand03/toenisvorst_wohnungsbrand/index.jhtml
2. Firegeezer Blog, Canada (2008),
   http://firegeezer.com/2008/05/02/ambulance-sent-to-wrong-city
3. Brocklehurst, E.: The NPL Electronic Paper Project. International Journal of Man-Machine Studies 34(1), 69–95 (1990)
4. Bier, E., Stone, M., Pier, K., Buxton, W., DeRose, T.: Toolglass and Magic Lenses: The See-through Interface. In: Proc. of SIGGRAPH 1993, pp. 73–80 (1993)
5. Schöning, J., Krüger, A., Müller, H.: Interaction of Mobile Camera Devices with Physical Maps. In: Adjunct Proc. of PERVASIVE 2006, pp. 121–124 (2006)
6. Golledge, R.G.: Geographical Perspectives on Spatial Cognition. Advances in Psychology 96, 16–46 (1993)
7. MacEachren, A., Brewer, I., Cai, G., Chen, J.: Visually Enabled Geocollaboration to Support Data Exploration and Decision-Making. In: Proc. of IIC 2003 (2003)
8. Florence, J., Hornsby, K., Egenhofer, M.: The GIS Wallboard: Interactions with Spatial Information on Large-scale Displays. In: International Symposium on Spatial Data Handling, vol. 7, pp. 449–463 (1996)

9. Oviatt, S.: Mulitmodal Interactive Maps: Designing for Human Performance. Human-Computer Interaction 12(1&2), 93–129 (1997)
10. Egenhofer, M.J.: Query Processing in Spatial-Query-by-Sketch. Journal of Visual Languages and Computing 8(4), 403–424 (1997)
11. Sharma, R., Poddar, I., Ozyildiz, E., Kettebekov, S., Kim, H., Huang, T.S.: Toward Interpretation of Natural Speech/Gesture: Spatial Planning on a Virtual Map. In: Proceedings of ARL Advanced Displays Annual Symposium, pp. 35–9 (1999)
12. Palen, L., Liu, S.: Citizen Communications in Crisis: Anticipating a Future of ICT–supported Public Participation. In: Proc. of CHI, pp. 727–736 (2007)
13. Yuan, Y., Detlor, B.: Intelligent mobile crisis response systems. Commun. ACM 48(2), 95–98 (2005)
14. Rohs, M., Schöning, J., Krüger, A., Hecht, B.: Towards Real-time Markerless Tracking of Magic Lenses on Paper Maps. In: LaMarca, A., Langheinrich, M., Truong, K.N. (eds.) Pervasive 2007. LNCS, vol. 4480, pp. 69–72. Springer, Heidelberg (2007)
15. Rohs, M., Schöning, J., Raubal, M., Essl, G., Krüger, A.: Map Navigation with Mobile Devices: Virtual versus Physical Movement with and without Visual Context. In: Proc. of ICMI 2007, pp. 146–153 (2007)
16. Baudisch, P., Rosenholtz, R.: Halo: A Technique for Visualizing Off-Screen Locations. In: Proc. CHI 2003, pp. 481–488 (2003)
17. Gustafson, S., Baudisch, P., Gutwin, C., Irani, P.: Wedge: clutter-free visualization of off-screen locations. In: CHI 2008: Proceeding of the twenty-sixth annual SIGCHI conference on Human factors in computing systems, pp. 787–796. ACM, New York (2008)
18. Hecht, B., Rohs, M., Schöning, J., Krüger, A.: WikEye–Using Magic Lenses to Explore Georeferenced Wikipedia Content. In: Proceedings of the 3rd International Workshop on Pervasive Mobile Interaction Devices (PERMID) (2007)
19. Schöning, J., Hecht, B., Starosielski, N.: Evaluating automatically generated location-based stories for tourists. In: CHI 2008: extended abstracts on Human factors in computing systems, pp. 2937–2942. ACM, New York (2008)
20. Schöning, J., Rohs, M., Krüger, A.: Mobile interaction with the real world. In: MIRW 2008: Workshop on Mobile Interaction with the Real World (2008)
21. Rath, O., Schöning, J., Rohs, M., Krüger, A.: Sight quest: A mobile game for paper maps. In: Intertain 2008: Adjunct Proceedings of the 2nd International Conference on INtelligent TEchnologies for interactive enterTAINment (2008)

Three-Way Pinpointing of Emergency Call from RFID-Reader-Equipped Cellular Phone

Osamu Takizawa[1], Masafumi Hosokawa[2], Ken'ichi Takanashi[3], Yasushi Hada[1], Akihiro Shibayama[1], and Byeong-pyo Jeong[1,3]

[1] Disaster Management and Mitigation Group, National Institute of Information and Communications Technology,
4-2-1, Nukuikita-machi, Koganei, Tokyo 184-8795, Japan
`{taki,had,shibayama,jeong}@nict.go.jp`
[2] Fire and Disaster Management Agency,
35-3, Jindaiji-Higashicho 4 chome, Chofu, Tokyo 182-8508, Japan
`hosokawa@fri.go.jp`
[3] National Research Institute of Fire and Disaster,
35-3, Jindaiji-Higashicho 4 chome, Chofu, Tokyo 182-8508, Japan
`takanasi@fri.go.jp`

Abstract. The ability to accurately pinpoint the point of origin of an emergency call can greatly increase response times of emergency services. Emergency calls made from cellular phones can only be traced by the Global Positioning System (GPS) or cell-based positioning, which are sometimes unacceptably inaccurate; they cannot provide information on, e.g. the exact floor of a building and also suffer from blind spots. We have been developing a system that can determine the location of a cellular phone using in-built passive or active radio-frequency identification (RFID) readers and GPS receivers. This paper introduces the outline of the prototype system.

Keywords: RFID, GPS, GIS, Cellular-phone, Emergency call.

1 Introduction

Emergency calls from cellular phones are becoming increasingly common. In Japan, from January to November 2006, 60% of emergency calls made to police stations originated from cellular phones; in FY 2002, around 20% of calls made to fire and ambulance stations originated from cellular phones.

In Japan, there are two serious problems concerning emergency calls from cellular phones to fire and ambulance stations. First, the calls must be routed to the fire department that has jurisdiction over the area where the call originated. A call from a cellular phone may be received by a base station in another region; and with over 800 fire departments, the emergency call can easily be routed to the wrong fire department. Second, even if the emergency call is connected to the correct fire department, the dispatcher must then be informed of the exact location of the emergency; and this may be difficult, especially when the call is being made by the person with the emergency. To solve these problems, GPS and cell-based positioning systems were introduced in

J. Löffler and M. Klann (Eds.): Mobile Response, LNCS 5424, pp. 66–75, 2009.
© Springer-Verlag Berlin Heidelberg 2009

fire departments across Japan in April 2007. However, cell-based positioning, available on any W-CDMA or CDMA2000 phones in Japan, is not sufficiently accurate for emergency calls. GPS positioning, available only on GPS-equipped devices, is more precise, but suffers from blind spots in, e.g. underground spaces and inside buildings; and moreover, GPS altitude information is not practical for our purposes, particularly in the absence of a clear view of the sky. In fire fighting and rescue, three-dimensional positioning is necessary to determine, e.g. which floor of an apartment buildings the call was made from. Therefore, we have been developing a system for determining the location of cellular phones by equipping them with passive or active radio-frequency identification (RFID) readers.

This work is supported in part through a research and development project called 'RFID-based Positioning Systems for Enhancing Safety and Sense of Security', promoted by the Japanese Ministry of Education, Culture, Sports, Science and Technology. This project is a collaborative effort involving the Center for Spatial Information Science of The University of Tokyo, the Geographical Survey Institute, the Fire and Disaster Management Agency, the National Research Institute of Police Science and the National Institute of Information and Communications Technology, Japan.

2   Overview of the Proposed System

RFID tags are of two types: active, incorporating a battery; and passive, not requiring a battery. A passive RFID tag modulates the carrier wave sent from the reader with the information in its storage area and returns the modulated wave back to the reader. In this case, the physical separation between the RFID tag and reader must be less than several centimetres; therefore, the reader must be consciously placed near the RFID tag. In contrast, active RFID tags have extended ranges and can actively transmit information, thus acting as beacons. Therefore, the reader does not have to be moved to establish communication with an active RFID tag. RFID tags used as positioning sources will have a positioning resolution determined by their communication range, when considering the possibility of interference from neighbouring RFID tags.

Our system comprises specially modified cellular phones (hereafter, terminals) and computer servers. The terminals are equipped with a passive RFID reader, an active RFID reader and a GPS receiver, thereby allowing three-way positioning. Position information from passive RFID tags must be read by placing the terminal near the tag, while active RFID tags will broadcast their information to any terminal within a 10–15-m radius. And in the absence of both, the terminal can always revert to conventional GPS or cell-based positioning, which have a positioning resolution of several tens of meters. Thus, in the proposed system, positioning accuracy is augmented by placing RFID tags particularly in GPS blind spots. Figure 1 shows an overview of the proposed system. In the figure, passive RFID tags are embedded in access control systems for doors, while active RFID tag are installed in residential fire alarms. The terminal, itself, functions as a personal ID card: The user places the terminal close to the access controller for the door, and the door opens if the user is authorized. At that moment, the terminal receives the room ID from the passive RFID tag on the door. Thus, the terminal is aware that the owner has entered a specific room. And if the user then makes an emergency call using the terminal, the room ID provides the user's position.

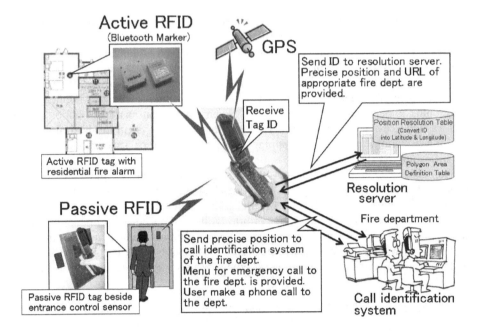

Fig. 1. Overview of proposed system

3 Outline of the Process

Figure 2 shows the sequence of processes in the proposed system in the case where the terminal has successfully received a positioning ID.

Process 1. The terminal first attempts to receive an ID from a passive RFID tag. The function of obtaining the room ID from a door, as described in the previous section, is still under development. Therefore, in the current system, passive RFID tags are assumed to be placed at conspicuous locations where emergency call would be made, e.g. near or on fire extinguishers. If this fails within a preset time period, the terminal begins to search for active RFID tags. And if this also within a preset time period, the terminal reverts to the GPS and cell-based positioning process, in which case a rough latitude and longitude are obtained. The terminal then sends the detected tag ID or latitude-longitude to a 'resolution server' via the available cellular packet network.

Process 2. The resolution server refers to a 'position resolution table' to convert the detected ID into an accurate latitude and longitude (Fig. 3). Each entry in the table consists of an ID, the corresponding latitude-longitude, the postal address and some remarks. This latitude-longitude information is used to search a 'polygon area definition table' for the URL of the correct fire department. Figure 4 shows an example polygon area definition table. Each field in the table includes the name of fire department, its URL and emergency phone number and its jurisdiction area defined by polygon of latitude-longitude pairs.

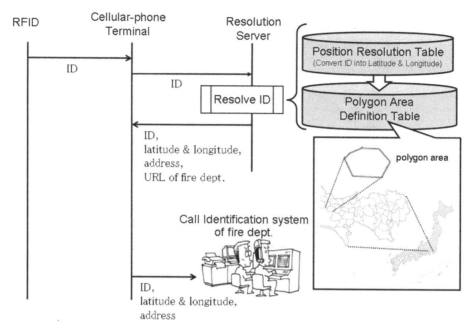

Fig. 2. Process sequence of proposed system

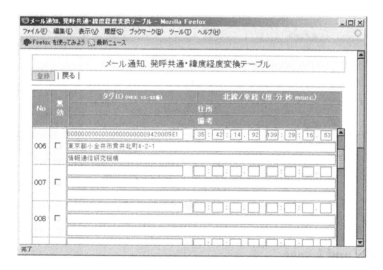

Fig. 3. Example position resolution table

Process 3. The terminal accesses the Web server whose URL is indicated in the polygon area definition table. The Web server provides a Web menu that provides options for selecting the emergency phone number or e-mail of the fire department for that area.

Process 4. The user selects the appropriate hyperlink on the Web menu to make the emergency phone call or send an e-mail.

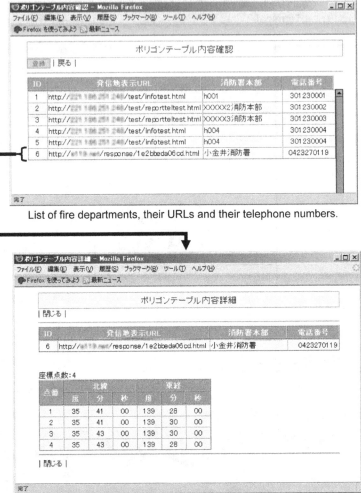

List of fire departments, their URLs and their telephone numbers.

An entry for a fire department with its jurisdiction defined by
a polygon bounded by latitude-longitude pairs.

Fig. 4. Example polygon area definition table

4 Details and Usage

Figure 5 shows an example terminal used in the proposed system. The main body
includes GPS and Bluetooth communication devices. A passive RFID reader is attached to the rear. Figures 6 and 7 show examples of passive and active RFID tags,
respectively. The active RFID tag is a commercial Bluetooth acceleration sensor. The
proposed system substitutes active RFID communication with Bluetooth.

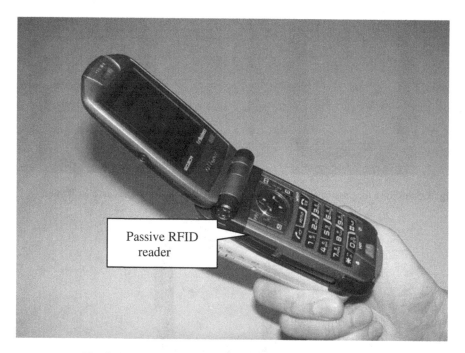

Fig. 5. Special cellular-phone terminal for the proposed system

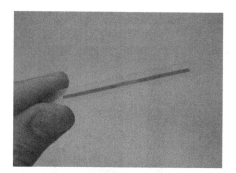

Fig. 6. Passive RFID tag   **Fig. 7.** Active RFID tag

Immediately after the system starts, the terminal attempts to connect to the passive RFID reader, and then begins to search for passive RFID tags (Fig. 8). If this search fails within a preset time period, the terminal begins to search for active RFID tags (Fig. 9). If it succeeds in obtaining the ID of a passive or active RFID tag, the terminal sends the ID to the resolution server (Fig. 10).

However, if the terminal fails to obtain any IDs, it reverts to the GPS or cell-based positioning processes (Fig. 11). The terminal obtains a rough latitude and longitude, which it sends to the resolution server (Fig. 12).

Fig. 8. Searching for passive RFID tags

Fig. 9. Searching for active RFID tags

Fig. 10. Sending ID to the resolution server

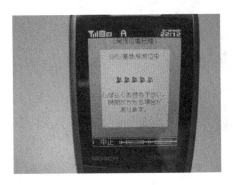

Fig. 11. GPS or cell-based positioning

Fig. 12. Sending the positioning results to the resolution server

When this process is complete, the terminal receives the URL of the appropriate fire department for that area from the resolution server. The terminal automatically accesses the URL and displays the Web menu of the fire department, which provides the option to call or e-mail the fire department (Fig. 13).

Selecting the hyperlink to call the fire department causes the phone to dial the preset telephone number of the appropriate fire department. When the emergency e-mail

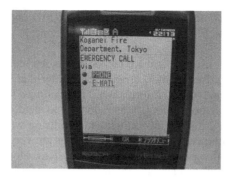

Fig. 13. Example Web menu of the fire department with jurisdiction over the area where the call originated. The menu provides hyperlinks for the emergency phone number or e-mail address.

hyperlink is selected, the e-mail address of the appropriate fire department is preset in the mail composer, and the terminal is ready for the user to compose and send an e-mail. This menu is not created by a terminal-dependent application but is hosted on a Web server. Therefore, this system is not restricted to specific models or makes of terminals, and the design of the Web menu can be easily modified.

The processing time from positioning to obtaining the telephone number or e-mail address is around 10 s.

5 Discussion

Many wireless location-based services (LBS) using RFID technology have been proposed. In most such services, persons carry active RFID tags, while readers form installed infrastructure. In such systems, the positions of tags are usually estimated by received signal strength indication (RSSI). In contrast, in our proposed system, RFID tags form the installed infrastructure, while the users carry readers. Our purpose is to identify the origin of an emergency call with a resolution sufficient to distinguishing between individual rooms in a building. Thus, simply receiving the RFID for the room is sufficient to identify the position. Moreover, if only one RFID tag is installed for several adjacent rooms, the room of origin can still be determined using RSSI. We have also performed a study on the use of RFID in searching for victims trapped by avalanches or collapsed structures [2]. The victims carried RFID tags and rescue team searched for them using RSSI. The results of that study will contribute to the development of the current system, if the positioning technology using RSSI is needed to be introduced in the system.

A typical location system in which RFID tags form the installed infrastructure, as in our system, is the proposed car navigation system in which multiple passive RFID tags are embedded on the road [3]. The purpose of our system is to ensure that emergency calls made from cellular phones in a specific region are routed to the dispatcher for the same region. Therefore, the resolution must be sufficient to allow identification of the specific room in which the terminal is located, or in other words, one active tag for one room. Active RFID tags are suitable for this purpose. Moreover, the combination of access-controlled doors and passive RFID tags makes it possible to identify the room in which a person is located. This concept for location systems is unique to our study.

A location system that uses general RF technology is the Indoor Messaging System (IMES) [4]. IMES comprises an indoor radio transmitter that sends GPS-compatible signals with position and other information. This allows GPS-equipped cellular phones to have seamless positioning both indoors and outdoors. Typical problems with IMES are the high costs the transmitters and collision with the real GPS signal from the satellites. In contrast to this, active RFID tags are very cheap, allowing them to be rapidly deployed; this is an advantage of our system. Moreover, if, through legislation or other means, all residential fire alarms are required to have built-in active RFID tags, the proposed location system will quickly become ubiquitous.

We now discuss the potential for cellular phones with built-in RFID readers to gain wide-spread acceptance. In the proposed system, active RFID is realized through Bluetooth technology. Therefore in our system, Bluetooth-equipped cellular phones, which are already quite common, are equivalent to phones with active RFID readers. In Europe, near field communication (NFC) technology, which has been standardized as ISO/IEC 18092, is already commercially available on cellular phones. This can be considered equivalent to the passive RFID readers used in our system (though unfortunately, NFC cellular phones are still not available in Japan [5]). In addition, NFC uses electromagnetic induction at 13.56 MHz to power the tags; this means that the tag and reader must be in contact. In contrast, our passive RFID system will use 2.45-GHz radio wave technology to power the tags, which allows some separation between tag and reader. Most applications of passive RFID systems involve of fixed readers and portable tags, where having to touch the tag with the reader is not very difficult. However, our system uses fixed tags and portable readers, where some separation should be allowed. Therefore, 2.45-GHz radio wave technology, not NFC, is suitable for our system.

In Japan, multifunctional cellular phones are quite popular; most come equipped with a camera, barcode reader, RFID chip and digital TV tuner. Therefore, in the near future, phones equipped with RFID readers may also become popular, given that appropriate applications are proposed. The Japanese Ministry of Internal Affairs and Communications created a research and development policy on 'ubiquitous platform technology' in FY 2008, which includes plans for the development of low-cost and robust RFID reader microchips for cellular phones.

In the proposed system, passive RFID tags are used as sources of position information. We have also studied the use of passive RFID for message boards and message exchange among citizens, and to provide information on buildings. The proposed system has already been realized on special PC-based terminal [2]. And if these functions can be realized on cellular phones, the system will, no doubt, see wide use.

6 Conclusion

We plan to perform a field experiment using the proposed system in FY 2008. One hurdle is the construction of a large-scale position resolution table for the resolution server. In the proposed system, the server is assumed to manage the data for *all* RFID tags. However, when a large number of RFID tags are deployed, such an intensive management is not realistic. In practice, we recommend the use of a distributed management system. Moreover, if a technical standard for RFID-based positioning systems for emergency calls is produces, many companies are expected to follow the standard and construct distributed infrastructure. Thus, even in practice, the fire department need not manage all tags and databases intensively.

Acknowledgments. The authors would like to thank Mr. Hiroyuki Fukuoka and Mr. Yoshifumi Shimazaki of KDDI R&D Laboratories Inc. for their support in developing the prototype system.

References

1. FDMA (in Japanese),
   http://www.fdma.go.jp/neuter/topics/jouhou/190126unyou.html
2. Takizawa, O., et al.: Hybrid Radio Frequency Identification System for Use in Disaster Relief as Positioning Source and Emergency Message Boards. In: Löffler, J., Klann, M. (eds.) Mobile Response 2007. LNCS, vol. 4458, pp. 85–94. Springer, Heidelberg (2007)
3. Chon, H.D., Jun, S., Jung, H., An, S.W.: Using RFID for Accurate Positioning. Journal of Global Positioning Systems 3, 32–39 (2004)
4. Satoshi, K., Hiroaki, M., Makoto, I., Dinesh, M., Kazuki, O.: The Concept of an Indoor Messaging System. European Navigation Conference (ENC-GNSS), G2A05-0271 (April 2008)
5. http://japan.internet.com (in Japanese), http://japan.internet.com/allnet/20071213/4.html

Capturing and Processing of 360° Panoramic Images for Emergency Site Exploration

Barbara Krausz[1], Andreas Brièll[2], Christian Eckes[1], and Jobst Löffler[1]

[1] Fraunhofer IAIS, Schloss Birlinghoven, 53754 Sankt Augustin, Germany
{Barbara.Krausz,Christian.Eckes,Jobst.Loeffler}@iais.fraunhofer.de
[2] iTouring GmbH, Dennewartstr. 25-27, 52068 Aachen, Germany
a.briell@itouring.de

Abstract. This paper describes the use of geo-referenced panoramic images for visual remote exploration in the SaR domain. It underlines the usefulness of panoramic images and distributed information services by presenting and discussing associated use cases. The complete workflow of capturing and processing of the panoramic images is described. Then a survey of approaches to post-processing, automatic analysis and visualization of panoramas is given and own results for automatic image analysis are presented. Finally, the features and components of information systems which provide functionality for retrieval and interactive visualization of geo-referenced panoramic images are described.

1 Introduction

The basic tools and information sources available to rescue forces during rescue operations today are, first, audio communication channels, second, paper maps of the site and fire protection maps of buildings affected, third, magnetic boards with tactical symbols used for resource planning, and finally, paper forms for command forwarding. If special information is required like the estimated risk caused by hazardous substances, human experts are requested by the officer in charge. The various information sources offered by public, commercial or official internet services are not or very rarely used in the field nowadays. The immense potential benefit that such online services could introduce to the operational work cannot be exploited because the reliable information infrastructure needed is not established to date. Furthermore, the services are often not known and not adapted to the special demands of the rescue forces.

This paper describes the use of 360° panoramic images captured along a close location grid of capturing points in residential areas. In section 1.1 possible use cases for emergency management for large-scale industry plants, for rescue operation management of city fire departments and for location-based services are presented and discussed. Afterwards, section 2 gives a survey of approaches to automatically processing and analyzing image data. In section 3 the commercial capturing and processing workflow originally used for touristic city visualization is presented in detail. This commercial system can be used in emergency management by adopting its technology (geo-referenced panorama images) and

J. Löffler and M. Klann (Eds.): Mobile Response, LNCS 5424, pp. 76–90, 2009.

deriving certain properties of the pictured environment. Own results of first experiments with algorithms for automatic analysis of the acquired panoramic images are described. The extracted building features such as window positions or the number of stories can be used to support various use cases with regard to emergency management. A geo-referenced information system which supports these use cases by giving access to panoramic images is introduced in the last section.

Finally, conclusions are drawn and an outlook to future developments with regard to emergency response is given.

1.1 Use Cases for Emergency Management

The following sections present use cases in which rescue forces benefit from panoramic images as an additional information source.

Emergency Management for Large-Scale Industrial Plants. In large-scale industrial plants like refineries it is often difficult to estimate on the basis of an abstract error message where the incident is located exactly and which risk potential arises from surrounding pipelines, containers, buildings etc.

By combining the digital visualization of the plant with the failure-management software one can get a high-resolution panorama of the incident environment in real-time without the need to explore the site. The possibility to judge the risk potential in a visual way speeds up the response time and therefore prevents further damages.

By distributing these visual data to all participating external emergency forces, which normally have small local knowledge, they can take a "local look around" before even being at the emergency site. This way the officer-in-charge can make initial decisions about the manpower and resources while still being in the head quarter.

Another possibility to use such a capturing unit is to mount autarkic units onto vehicles or robots which can autonomously explore sites which are unaccessible for humans. These panoramic images can help to get a better visual understanding of the location. It is also easier to direct the robot or to operate its instruments.

The digital visualization of an industrial plant supports the internal and external emergency forces within their reaction- and decision-processes and therefore can help to minimize the arising damage.

Digital City Image for Remote Exploration by Fire Brigades. The visualization of a complete city will create visual content, which can be used by the city government for many opportunities, especially for the city fire brigade.

The major use for the fire brigade comes from the possibility to access high resolution, spatial visual data of the emergency site, without exploring the site. This way the officer-in-charge can have a look at the houses affected by an accident and their surrounding immediately. This helps making decision for different aspects, e.g.

- How many men are necessary?
- Which vehicles are needed?
- Is the street wide enough for big vehicles?
- Where is the next fire hydrant?
- Is there a high-risk potential coming from the environment?

Also the heaviness of the damage caused can be estimated by a visual comparison of the building before and after an accident. These and many more aspects can be discussed even before leaving the fire department and therefore help to being prepared even better.

On the way to the emergency site panorama and map data help to explore the surrounding environment. This will minimize reaction times after arriving at the emergency site.

Vehicles equipped with a capturing unit can take panoramic images of the emergency site and transfer them to the mobile command post where these image can support the officer-in-charge. For that purpose, the capturing unit has to act independently so that no firefighter has to interact or operate the capturing unit. As mentioned before, it is also possible to mount such a capturing unit onto a robot which can autonomously explore an emergency site which is unaccessible for humans.

Next-Generation Car Navigation Systems / Location-Based Services.
Besides emergency management, the acquired data can also be used to offer a next-generation car navigation system as proposed for example by Cornelis et al. [1]. Such a system offers the possibility to visualize the environment with the help of 3D models of the buildings which enables the driver to easily navigate through a city and to foresee difficult traffic situations. Again such kind of services can be used by rescue forces for optimal route planning for the units approaching the operation site.

2   Survey of Image Processing Approaches

After having acquired images such as panorama images as described in section 3, this data can be utilized in order to support the use cases mentioned in section 1.1 in several ways: Firstly, the data can be visualized. For example a three-dimensional model of the pictured buildings can be recovered and visualized. This would be helpful for a fire brigade for example in order to see, if there are other buildings next to a burning house or where there are entrances into this building. Another possibility of visualizing the acquired data is a two-dimensional panorama view.

Secondly, the images can automatically be analyzed to segment the image or derive certain properties of the pictured scene, for example locating buildings, persons or traffic signs. In contrast to the reconstruction of three-dimensional models, approaches for automatic analysis try to associate regions of an image with semantic information. Information about buildings such as the height of a building, the number of floors and the number of adjacent buildings can be useful for emergency management as described above. However, now this information is derived automatically.

The following section gives an overview of works in these fields.

2.1   2D Panorama Views from Video

Rescue forces can benefit from 2D panorama view as they can get a rough impression of an emergency site. They can estimate the dimensions of a building or locate entrances or risk potentials.

An automatic system for the creation of panorama views from a video sequence captured from a moving vehicle is proposed in [15]. In each frame a vertical line at a fixed position is extracted and stitched together with vertical lines of successive frames to obtain a consecutive two-dimensional image. This route panorama exhibits an orthogonal projection along the camera path and a perspective projection along the vertical direction. In route panoramas distant objects are extended horizontally, whereas objects closer to the camera appear narrower or might even disappear.

Agarwala et al. [16] propose a system that processes semi-automatically a series of photographs taken from multiple viewpoints (distance between viewpoints approx. 1m) with a handheld still-camera. Firstly, the camera positions and orientations are recovered using structure-from-motion. Afterwards, the user defines a picture surface, which should be roughly aligned with the scenes dominant plane. This picture surface will contain the resulting panorama. Each sample on this picture surface is located in the source photographs and its final pixel value is computed by considering some basic properties that a panorama view should exhibit. For example an object should be pictured from a viewpoint almost in front of it.

2.2   360° Panoramas from Synchronized Still Images

A 360° panoramic image offers the possibility to have a "local look around" from the viewpoint the panoramic image has been created. If several panoramic images are available, the user can even "walk" around and see a building from different viewpoints. Note that in this case buildings are not constructed and no 3D models of buildings are obtained. With this type of panoramic images rescue forces can get an adequate impression of the whole environment of an emergency site. They can even see the opposing buildings of a burning house for example.

Section 3 will describe the capturing and processing of 360° panoramic images in detail.

2.3   3D Models from Photographs

In contrast to the afore mentioned possibilities to process acquired image data, 3D models offer additional information to rescue forces. For example, with 3D models measurements (e.g. dimension of buildings) can be done, since buildings are reconstructed. Rescue forces might even be able to see details of a building which are not visible from the street.

One example for the construction of three-dimensional models is the system Façade [13]. Few photographs are needed to build up a model of the pictured building in a semi-automatic manner. Firstly, the user constructs a basic geometrical model by combining volumetric primitives such as boxes or wedges. Furthermore, the user marks edges in the two-dimensional images and their corresponding edges in the model. The system then reconstructs unknown model parameters and camera positions by minimizing a cost function that takes into account the differences between projected edges and their corresponding marked edges. A realistic view of the building from arbitrary viewpoints can then be computed by superimposing original photographs onto the model, since the camera positions of the photographs have been reconstructed. The basic model is further improved by recovering geometric details. For that purpose, model-based stereo is utilized, that is the basic model is used as a priori information and compared to the actual scene. Corresponding points in two images are found by projecting a point onto the basic model of the building, viewing it from the viewpoint of the camera position of the second photograph and comparing this with the corresponding point in the second image.

A recent project for reconstruction of urban scenes is UrbanScape [14]. This project aims at reconstructing geo-registered three-dimensional models. Eight video cameras (30 Hz) are mounted on the top of a car, which is equipped with a GPS/INS system. In a sparse reconstruction step, the correspondences between points in consecutive frames are established. After that, camera positions are recovered in terms of 3D world coordinates. These coordinates are then transferred to geo-registered coordinates with the help of the GPS/INS system. In a dense reconstruction step, a single video stream and the camera poses are analyzed using a plane-sweep algorithm to output a depth map for each frame. Multiple depth maps of successive frame are then fused to improve depth estimates by taking consistency between depth maps into account. From these depth maps, a texture-mapped three-dimensional model in geo-registered coordinates is generated.

2.4   Automatic Image Analysis for Building Feature Extraction

Besides recovering 3D models or constructing panorama views, one can also analyze the acquired data automatically in order to support the use cases mentioned in section 1.1. There is few work in automatic processing and deriving properties of buildings from ground view images. However, there are many projects dealing with aerial images which are not considered in this survey.

Trinh et al. [17] detect line segments together with dominant vanishing points in an image. Certain properties of line segments belonging to a building are then analyzed to reject line segments not being part of a building. For example, line segments are parallel and often occur alongside with a distance between them that is proportional to their length. The proposed algorithms are used to classify images into building or non-building images. Furthermore, facets of buildings can be detected by examining detected line segments.

Berg et al. [18] segment the image into building regions, sky, street and foliage. In a learning stage probabilities for these categories are modeled by estimating how often a certain feature co-occurs with a category. The system includes features such as color histogram, contour, texturedness and position. Additionally, Berg et al. locate particular elements of buildings, e.g. windows, doors, roof etc. in the images. For that purpose, linear structure detectors as well as right angle and t-junctions detectors are utilized.

Approaches like Müller et al. [19], Mayer and Reznik [20] or Dick et al. [21] combine the reconstruction of three-dimensional models with automatic analysis.

3 Capturing of Panoramic Images

Mapping and visualizing the reality is a trend not only in scientific research and development ([2], [3], [4]) but also in broad public. Most notable result is Google Maps. The level of visualization these tools offer via Internet is much more detailed and comprehensive than anybody would have expected a few years ago.

Today the best level of detail is achieved by high-resolution satellite images [5], which show a sub-meter precise map-based view of the earth. The third dimension is not yet that detailed, as first 3D cities in Google Maps show. Being able to see the world from a pedestrian perspective with a detail level that feels like "being local", is the next big thing to come.

Virtual tours based on panorama photographs try to achieve this since the end of the 90s with a low technology approach [6]. Manual data capturing and processing is still state-of-the-art for the majority of virtual tour vendors. A new basic technology is necessary to improve these processes and finally achieve the aim of a three dimensional high detailed visualization of the reality.

Such a new basic technology for the production and presentation process of panorama-based virtual tours has been developed in a previous project by the iTouring GmbH. iTouring tours – so called digital interactive tours (diTours) – offer a digital visualization of the reality by means of high resolution 360° panorama photographs. The viewer can navigate freely within a dense location grid in this "digital world". Thousands of linked panoramas provide the possibility to visualize buildings, plants, cities or islands not just fractional but as a whole, with just a fraction of the time compared to common approaches.

In the following this commercial system originally developed for touristic purposes is described in detail.

3.1 Software Components

The main key-component of the iTouring technology is the software-based "iTouring Processing System" (iTPS) (see figure 1). It allows to process captured position and picture data full automatically. The processing time is in real-time and better. This allows immediate utilization of the processed data and therefore short reaction times.

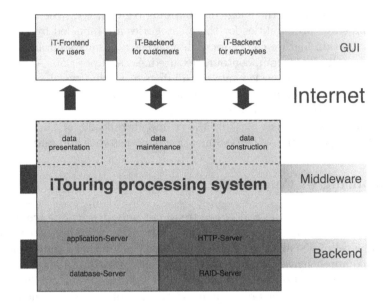

Fig. 1. iTPS basic structure

The iTPS has been developed according to the principle of the 3-tier-architecture, which has been established as mayor basic structure for web-based applications. User interface, business logic and backend are clearly separated from each other, making the iTPS flexible and high-performance.

The entire iTPS is based on standardized Internet technologies and each tour production step is accessible via secure Internet connection. All servers are redundantly designed. Hence, the application-, database- and web-servers are highly available and load balancers provide optimal performance even under heavy user loads.

3.2 Hardware Components

Beside the iTPS software there is one hardware key-component, which is essential for the iTouring technology, the "iTouring Capturing System" (iTCS). This vehicle-based unit allows capturing position and picture data very fast and reliable. Simply by driving through a given terrain it allows capturing high-resolution panoramas in a dense grid. This data is transferred to the iTouring data center and processed by the iTPS full automatically. The result is a high-resolution geo-referenced panorama tour of the terrain.

The iTCS shows similarities to Mobile Mapping Vehicles (MMVs), which have recently been developed at universities ([7], [8], [2]) and private companies in order to economize the data capturing and maintenance process, especially for mapping and navigation business. The iTCS uses the same main components as common MMVs:

- INS/GPS
- Odometer
- Cameras

But there are also some major differences, as the iTCS is designed as a

- low-cost
- small-sized
- modular
- spherical

system. The most obvious difference is the size, which allows using small cars instead of big vans for the iTCS.

The iTCS is based on five main components, which are attached to the central processing unit as shown in figure 2. The picture capturing unit comprises four high-performance high-resolution CCD-cameras, which are combined with special fisheye lenses. This unit is able to deliver high-resolution 10 MPixel spherical panoramas at a speed of up to five panoramas per second. This allows high capturing speed even with a small grid basis length of a few meters. A typical problem when capturing visual data when moving is the low dynamic range most common picture sensors offer. The iTCS uses a dual-camera per view approach to capture the same scene with different exposure times and afterwards combining these two images with common HDR procedures as shown in [10] and [11].

The INS (Inertial Navigation Unit) delivers high precise position data even under difficult conditions like urban canyon situations or tunnels. The average error is less than 1m for the two-dimensional absolute position determination. The average error of the relative position determination between the capturing-grid basis length is less than 1% of the basis length, which is just a few centimeters. This high precise position information upvalues the picture data since use cases can be accomplished which need very accurate position information (e.g. photogrammetry).

The navigation module is designed as a "digital copilot" that directs the driver through the terrain to be captured. A special navigation algorithm, based on the

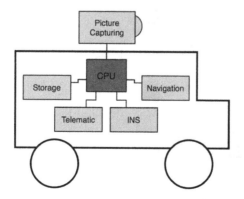

Fig. 2. iTCS hardware setup

"Chinese postman problem" [12], calculates the shortest tour through the street network of a given terrain while all streets must be covered at least once.

The movement of the iTCS is not just captured and saved but also transferred to the company's headquarter by the telematic module. This way the fleet operator knows exactly where each iTCS unit is at a certain time point. Furthermore, additional information is transferred, which helps to determine problems immediately after or even before they arise. This helps to increase the uptime and productivity of each unit.

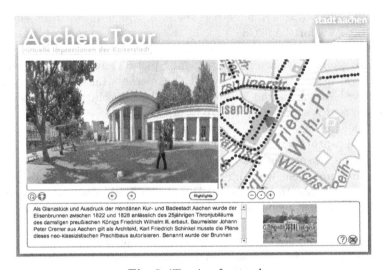

Fig. 3. iTouring frontend

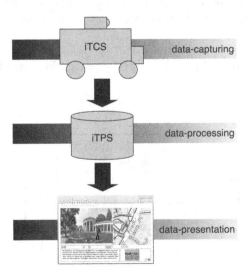

Fig. 4. 3-step visualization workflow

The acquired data is processed by the CPU (central processor unit) and afterwards stored in the mobile storage pool. This storage pool contains several 2,5" hard disk drives, which can endure vibrations caused by the driving process much better than 3,5" drives. To handle hard drive failures during the capturing process without stopping the drive, the storage is designed as a RAID 15. This RAID level combines data mirroring for best possible data security and data parity for best possible uptime. Depending on the demands of a given project, this storage pool can be sized up to several terabytes for daily captured data.

3.3 Visualization

The visualization workflow is based on the two described components iTCS and iTPS, which represent the data-capturing and data-processing level of the workflow. In addition the data-presentation level is accomplished by the iTouring frontend, a web browser based rich Internet application (RIA) client, as shown in figure 3.

This user frontend combines the panorama picture with its geo-position in a map. Furthermore, it illustrates the active "field of view" of the panorama within the map by means of a red triangle.

The whole visualization workflow is accomplished in three steps, as shown in figure 4. Due to the high automation this process-flow is very fast and can even be fulfilled in real-time on demand. In this case the data transport between the three processing-levels must be wireless and without any interruption. This can be accomplished by means of wireless 3G networks, which are already available today.

4 Processing and Automatic Analysis of Panoramic Images for Building Feature Extraction

As mentioned above, panoramic images can also be analyzed automatically in order to associate certain regions of an image with semantic information. For example, a building with its elements (door, windows and balconies) can be located. With this information the number of floors, the positions of entrances, the number of adjacent buildings and optionally the number of people living in a house could be determined automatically which is useful for emergency management.

In our project we have conducted some experiments in locating windows in the images. After having detected some windows, this information can be used to segment buildings, as mostly windows of different buildings are of different type or have different heights and positions.

In the current implementation first a rectilinear view is extracted from the equirectangular panorama with the help of the Panorama Tools [22], see figure 5. Afterwards, an abstract version of an input image is obtained by means of a dual rank filter according to Eckstein and Munkelt [23]. Thereby, details of a window as vertical or horizontal bars are eliminated and windows appear as an almost homogeneous area. In the next step thresholding with several different thresholds is performed. In each thresholded image rectangular structures are searched for. For each rectangle a score based on typical aspect ratios of windows and some other properties of rectangles is computed. Figure 5b shows the result of this analysis. The recognition rate is still not perfect but promising. In our first experiments we found false positives as well as false negatives which have to be reduced. A detailed evaluation has to be made in a next step.

After having located some windows, a model of the façade is constructed using the knowledge that regions lying between two windows belong to the façade. Two different approaches for creating a model have been tested: a Gaussian Mixture Model (GMM) and SIOX. For the GMM approach an unsupervised learning algorithm has been used [24]. Such a model is built up for the façade of a building using pixels lying between two windows. Furthermore, a GMM is created for modeling the street. Each pixel of the image is then compared with these models. If the log-likelihood (see [24]) for belonging to a façade class or the street class is less than a certain threshold, this pixel is classified as façade or as street, respectively. See figure 6(a) for an example of the classification using Gaussian Mixture Models.

The second approach uses SIOX (Simple Interactive Object Extraction, [25]). Originally, SIOX was developed as an interactive tool to segment an image and has recently been integrated into GIMP. Usually, the user has to define some foreground and background regions interactively. In our tests, we have used it to automatically segment the image. For that purpose, we define windows as belonging to the background and regions between windows as foreground classes. For each class a signature using the CIELab color space is created and in the classification stage the Euclidean distances of a pixel to all classes is calculated. The pixel is then assigned to the class with the lowest distance. See [25] for a detailed description of the algorithm and figure 6(b) for an example of the classification.

Our first experiments for automatic segmenting were promising as can be seen from figure 6(a) and 6(b). However, we have not yet compared the two different approaches in terms of false negatives or false positives.

5   A Conceptual Sketch of a Geo-Referenced Information System for Visual Remote Exploration

In order to provide access to the panoramic images to end-users, an information service is needed that supports search by address or position and delivers matching panoramas over a network. A client application for visual remote exploration can then request such a service and provides interactive visualization functionality. The following processes and components are needed to set up such an information system:

– Linking of addresses with geo-referenced panoramas using geo-data
– Automatic metadata generation and indexing

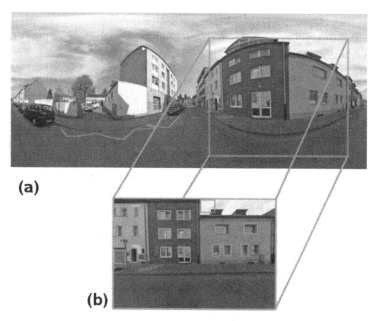

Fig. 5. (a) Equirectangular panorama, (b) rectilinear view and automatic detection of windows (image source: iTouring)

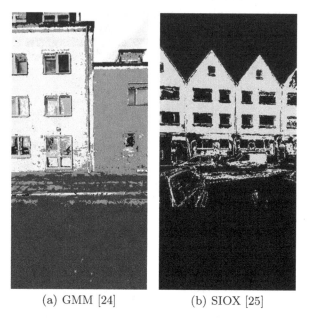

(a) GMM [24]   (b) SIOX [25]

Fig. 6. Examples for classification using GMMs and SIOX for modelling the façade. (image source: iTouring).

– Storage component
– Retrieval service: search by address or position
– Retrieval client: retrieval, visualization of geo-referenced panoramas together
  with results of automatic analysis

We described a mobile information and comunication system for large-scale
rescue operations in [26]. The distributed collaborative SHARE system comprises
the following components: a digital operation map with annotation functionality, an intelligent ressource management tool, audio/video/text communication
tools and a retrieval system for multimedia communication messages. The digital operation map provides location-based services which can be used to display
valuable information within a radius around the user's position for instance all
hospitals near the operation site. Multimedia information like additional fire rescue plans of buildings can be superimposed as map layer using the map client.

A concept for an extension for the SHARE system which allows retrieval and
display of panoramic images for the emergency site can be based on the service-
oriented architecture approach. By clicking on a certain position on the map
the user requests a panorama for that location. The SHARE system then sends
a request to the panoramic images retrieval service which send the matching
panorama back to the SHARE client application. Figure 7 shows a conceptual
sketch of the SHARE map client application with a panorama for a selected
location on the map.

The decribed solution can be used for remote exploration of the emergency site
from the main fire station before first units are sent to the site. In the field the
officer-in-charge can use the SHARE map client to explore the surroundings. A

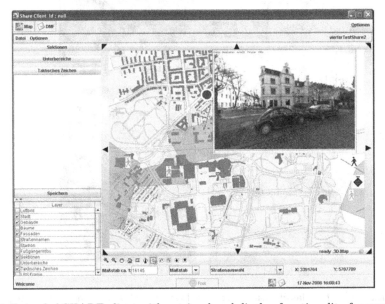

Fig. 7. Extended SHARE client with retrieval and display functionality for panoramic
images

comparison of a building before and after the accident will be done by using automatic image analysis which can provide valuable information about the dimensions of the situation.

6 Conclusion

This paper presented use cases for panoramic images and information services and described the capturing, processing, automatic analysis and visualization of panoramic images. Features and components for information services which provide retrieval and interactive visualization functionality were described. Finally, a concept for the integration in an existing information and communication system for rescue forces were explained. This concept will be implemented and evaluated in future projects.

References

1. Cornelis, N., Cornelis, K., Van Gool, L.: Fast Compact City Modeling for Navigation Pre-Visualization. In: IEEE Conf. on Computer Vision and Pattern Recognition, pp. 1339–1344 (2006)
2. Cameron, E., Naser, E.: Land-based Mobile Mapping Systems. Photogrammetric engineering and remote sensing, 13–28 (2002)
3. Hild, H.: Automatic Image-To-Map-Registration of Remote Sensing Data. In: Photogrammetric Week 2001, pp. 13–23. Herbert Wichmann Verlag, Heidelberg (2001)
4. Chen, S.E.: QuickTime VR - An Image-Based Approach to Virtual Environment Navigation. In: Proceedings of the 22nd annual conference on computer graphics and interactive techniques SIGGRAPH 1995, vol. 29 (1995)
5. Corbley, K.P.: Geoeye-1 Satellize coming. GEOconnexion International Magazine, 50–55 (2006)
6. Panoguide.com, Panorama creation tutorials (last access: March 2008), http://www.panoguide.com/howto/
7. Gräfe, G.: Erfahrungen bei der kinematischen Erfassung von Verkehrswegen mit MoSES. In: 14th International Conference on Engineering Surveying, Zürich (2004)
8. Benning, W.: Mobile mapping by a car driven survey system (CdSS). In: The International Symposium on Kinematic System, Geodesy, Geomatics and Navigation (1998)
9. TeleAtlas: We're mapping your world (last access: March 2008), www.teleatlas.com/WhyTeleAtlas/FAQs/ssLINK/TA_CT012494
10. Höreth, M.: Tone-Mapping Verfahren zur Darstellung von High Dynamic Range Bildern. Studienarbeit Universitt Koblenz-Landau (2003)
11. Kuipers, T.: HDRI - High Dynamic Rage Imaging. Seminarvortrag TU Clausthal (2007)
12. Gibbons, A.: Algorithmic Graph Theory. Cambridge University Press, Cambridge (1985)
13. Debevec, P., Taylor, C., Malik, J.: Modeling and rendering architecture from photographs: a hybrid geometry- and image-based approach. In: Proceedings of SIGGRAPH 1996, pp. 11–20 (1996)

14. Akbarzadeh, A., et al.: Towards Urban 3D Reconstruction from Video. In: Third International Symposium on 3D Data Processing, Visualization, and Transmission, pp. 1–8 (2006)
15. Zheng, J.: Digital route panoramas. IEEE Multimedia 10, 57–67 (2003)
16. Agarwala, A., et al.: Photographing long scenes with multi-viewpoint panoramas. ACM Trans. Graph. 25, 853–861 (2006)
17. Trinh, H., Kim, D., Jo, K.: Urban Building Detection by Visual and Geometrical Features. In: International Conf. on Control, Automation and Systems, pp. 1779–1784 (2007)
18. Berg, A., Grabler, F., Malik, J.: Parsing Images of Architectural Scenes. In: IEEEInternational Conference on Computer Vision, pp. 1–8 (2007)
19. Müller, P., Zeng, G., Wonka, P., Van Gool, L.: Image-based procedural modeling of façades. ACM Trans. Graph. 26 (2007)
20. Mayer, H., Reznik, S.: Building Faade Interpretation from Image Sequences. CMRT 36, 55–60 (2005)
21. Dick, A., Torr, P., Cipolla, R.: Modelling and Interpretation of Architecture from Several Images. Int. J. Comput. Vision 60, 111–134 (2004)
22. Panorama Tools, `http://panotools.sourceforge.net`
23. Eckstein, W., Munkelt, O.: Extracting Objects from Digital Terrain Models. Remote Sensing and Reconstruction for Three-Dimensional Objects and Scenes (1995)
24. Bouman, C.A.: Cluster: An unsupervised algorithm for modeling Gaussian mixtures, `http://www.ece.purdue.edu/~bouman`
25. Friedland, G., Jantz, K., Knipping, L., Rojas, R.: Image Segmentation by Uniform Color Clustering – Approach and Benchmark Results Technical Report B-05-07, Department of Computer Science, Freie Universitaet Berlin (2005), `www.siox.org`
26. Löffler, J., Schon, J., Hernandez Ernst, V., Pottebaum, J., Koch, R.: Intelligent Use of Geospatial Information for Emergency Operation Management. In: Proceedings of ISCRAM 2007 conference (2007)

Context Dependant Mobile Interfaces
for Collaboration
in Extreme Environment

Bernard Pavard[1], Fabrice Gourbault[2], and Cedric Mouton[2]

[1] Cognitive Engineering group, IRIT, UPS, France
[2] SCRIPTAL
www.sciptal.com

Abstract. The aim of this paper is to describe a wireless cooperative system that has been specifically designed to improve medical collaboration in a degraded environment such as battle field, crisis or major disaster. We will focus on three points: the structural field data analysis we used to specify the interface, the multi agent and virtual reality simulation platforms we used in order to assess the usability of the cooperative technology and the final field test where we ran an operational scenario to assess the system.

Keywords: agile, cooperation, interfaces, mobile.

1 Introduction

Collaboration in extreme environments seems to challenge organizational theories as well as design methodologies due to the fact that in most cases, communication infrastructures are out of work, organizations may be strongly impaired and actors (stakeholders) are confronted to a high level of social, psychological and cultural stress (Jennex 2007; Yang and Rothkrantz 2007).

If we take the Information Management point of view of this problem, we are facing in most cases, situations where the knowledge is incomplete, rapidly out of date and distributed over actors that are difficult to contact. Individual representations may also be perturbed and stakeholders rarely share the same point of view and the same interest.

Recent surveys made in national and international agencies in charge of emergency management (ONU, CICR, OCHA, PAM, etc.) pointed out the fact that problems are recurrent in most of such situations (Pavard, 2007). In all crisis situations we can observe problems concerning:

- *Language*: difficulties to communicate with local actors
- *Data quality*: good information is mandatory in the disaster and recovery phases but infrastructure and communications are often impaired and communications are not always reaching coordinators.
- *Coordination*: information is of high value in the first phase of the crisis and stakeholders may be reluctant to share it (high money value)

J. Löffler and M. Klann (Eds.): Mobile Response, LNCS 5424, pp. 91–100, 2009.

- *Personal security*:   More and more medical actors are themselves at risk in a conflict situation.
- *Technological flexibility*: depending of the countries, technologies may or may not be authorized (specifically sat com, GPS, etc.). In such conditions it is mandatory to have a real interoperability between communication technologies as well as software tools (HF, VHF, Sat, data, voice, etc.).

Helping people to collaborate in extreme environment thus needs a specific approach. In such situations formal organizations have problems to cope with uncertainty, lack of information, network disruption, etc. (Thomson 1967). In crisis situations cooperation is often informal, spontaneous in character and omnipresent. It is composed of group of interest and personal relationships. Occasionally it performs functions for the formal organization in which it develops (Chislom 1989).

In such situations stakeholders are usually geographically distributed, temporally disconnected to their hierarchy which is in most cases is under informed. In such situation we can often observe emergent cooperation between local stockholders.

This situation raises also a theoretical debate: how can we combine classical organizational centralized concepts (which looks at optimal formal organizations) and distributed, emergent cooperation which is based on opportunistic local interactions, plan reformulation, etc. This problem has been tentatively formalized in the context of high risk organization (Grote, 2007), multi organizational systems (Chisholm 1989), agile management (Atkinson and Moffat 2005, Harrold 2006) or crisis management (Pavard et al. 2007, Steele and Pariès, 2007).

In this paper we will focus on the methodology we used to design a communication system that could work both in normal and degraded situation. This system should:

- Help stakeholders to collaborate locally in order to promote *new emergent forms* of organization and,
- Help coordinator to rapidly share information with their field workers to find the best synergies.

This paper will focus on two points:

1)   A systemic methodology that allows the designer to specify user needs in extreme situations (very close to traditional approaches in HF but we pushed this approach to a formalization process that allows us to systematically test how new functionalities will cover the stakeholders needs).
2)   The use of simulation to assess the usability of new technologies.

The theoretical background of our approach based on the notion of crisis situation seen as a combination of emergent and structured organization (Pavard et al. 2007).

2 Project's Description

The project concerns the design of an information technology that can be used to improve coordination in case of extremely degraded situations. We are concerned both by civil and military applications. In the case of the military application, we had to take into account some specific particularities: all actors (military stakeholders) are wearing their own medical database (RFID tags) and may be exposed to situations where displacements are constrained by a strategic war plan.

The civil application may also share with the military one some comparisons like exposition to personal risks but usually they are less constrained by spatial displacement (but in case of environmental particularities like with earthquakes, massive traffic jams, etc.).

3 Methodology

Two methodologies have been used to assess user needs. The first one has been used for our civil application (middle scale emergency management) and was mainly based on ethnographic observations during annual exercises (Pavard & al., 2007). Due to the specificity of the military situation (military conflict, major crisis) it was not possible to do ethnographical but an alternative approach has been used. We ran collective expert interviews with operational teams that came back from several missions in different foreign countries. These interviews were intentionally open. We just focused the interviewees to give us examples of situations they encounter when doing their medical expertise in the battle field. In our case, experts came naturally to a storytelling mode that gives a good opportunity to contextualize user requirements. The point we would like to focus on in this paper is the systemic dimension of our analysis: how we went from open interviews to converge to functional and technical specifications.

We ran three interviews with teams (5 to 7 persons per teams) that were going back from difficult military missions in foreign countries.

Those expert teams were medics, health military worker or paramedics and the discussion was concerning only the mission they had been recently sent.

For each interviewee, raw linguistic material was integrally reported from which we extracted short sentences before to be formalized to fit a database :

Extract from a Medic interview:

   Actor (medic), *Country* (Ivory Coast) *Context* (City conflict)

   (1) During difficult conflicts in foreign countries we may override our medical duties
- Paramedics may help to perfuse
- We medically take care of civilians

   (2) Trust in our colleagues and the technology is more important than anything else

   (3) If I trust my paramedic, he will behave as I do in case I am too tired or if transmissions failed.

   (4) It is difficult to handle hierarchical requests. They want to know everything on the situation.

   (5) It is sometimes very difficult to make a clear cut between medical and military activities. When we send information about the victims, it is also strategic information for both us and the enemy.

   (6) Difficulties arise as soon as we want to know something about the victims.

   (7) We often loose contact with the command and control center but on the front side, we still need to know what we are doing, what is the situation.

(8) I usually do not have enough time to prepare my medical wallet (in order to fit it to the situation) before to leave my tent.

(9) I'd rather prefer to have a vocal contact from my paramedic than any message or picture.

(10) If the communications are not so good, SMS (Short Text Messages) may go through, not the voice.

(11) On the battle field, I never use medical sheets, never.

(12) Sometimes it is very difficult to remember where the victims are (specifically during the night). If we had a GPS it would have been easier.

From this first raw data collection, we categorized the user needs following *technical categories*.

Concerning the category *'Technological transparency '*, we ended with items like:

N1: Need of technological transparency (invisibility, ease of use)

(Technological transparency characterizes the fact that in the context of military action, the user interface should not be intrusive or difficult to use. It should work naturally in the flow of actions).

From the previous example, we could isolate several sentences:

(9) I'd rather prefer to have a vocal contact from my paramedic than any message or picture.

(10) If the communications are not so good, SMS (Short Text Messages) may go through, not the voice.

Finally, we ended with a database like:

Need (Techno Transparency, Expression [4], Nature [No cost interfaces])

[4] refer to the sentences 4 in the interviews.

This database formalization helps us to know the needs (techno transparency, etc.) and who was referring to this need (medics, paramedics, etc.). Subsequently, after technical specification we will use this database to check out if the technical specifications could fit all the needs.

N2 : Need of geospatial information

Geospatial information concerning the position of the victims or dangerous sites is mandatory because sometimes it is difficult to track back victim and to avoid dangers. Medics may also need to know where the paramedics are in order to plan their future actions.

Database expression:

Need (Geolocalisation, Expression [12], Nature [Common map, Individual scaling])

N3 : Need to manage degraded modes

There is a strong link between degraded modes and communication architecture. In crisis situation, the communication may degrade for many reasons: lost of contact with the coordination center, lost of communication terminal, danger, high workload, etc. In such situation, it is mandatory that rescue workers (localized in the front field) can still locally communicate between themselves to locally collaborate. From a functional point of view, the future communication network will need to be enough robust to maintain a basic level of communication between workers on the site.

Database expression:
Need (Degraded modes, Expression [7,10,12], Nature [Network architecture (Peer/Peer, Interoperability])

N4 : Need of context dependant interfaces

This requirement is mandatory both for civil and military applications. As an example, depending of the situation, the same information must be sent either by voice or text. If the environment is too noisy or with a poor communication performance, it will be better to use either written annotation or short messages (which are more immune to low signal/noise than voice communication.

Database expression:
Need (Context dependant interfaces, Expression [10], Nature [multimodality, Interoperability])

Other explored needs were: *continuity of services (ubiquity), interoperability, improving a common vision, cooperation between medics and paramedics.*

The last step of this approach was to go from functional specification (N1, N2, etc.) to technical specification (what is the technology that fit the best the user needs?).
This work has been done in collaboration with the engineers in order to find a solution that will allows us to satisfy all requests present in our database.
In order to assess the technological specification (prior to prototype it), we used 1) the database to check out if provided functionalities were covering all user needs, a multi agent and a virtual world simulation.

4   Technical Specification: The Concept of 'Extreme Interface'

Following this extensive user need analysis, it becomes clear that any technological solution where the paramedics or the medics mandatorily have to type information and loose time would be desperately unusable.
The medical military activity (like probably all other emergency activities) is context dependant. For example, in some situations actors will need to be very quiet and use only written or typed information and in other they will have to send the same information but only vocally.
These constraints drive us towards the concept of spatially localized container by analogy with a container for the video codec's (Fig. 1).

Fig. 1. The concept of container: as soon as the medic is close to the victim, the RFID reader captures the victim personal data. Any forthcoming multimodal data (vocal comments, picture, hand written or typed information) is then sent either to the central server or to the local colleagues. All data are visible by everybody and accessible from the map.

Terminals have GPS sensors to capture the spatial coordinates and multimedia information (voice, text, pictures, etc.) that are taken where the victim has been localized are stored in this virtual container that can be localized on a map from an icon (Fig. 2).

Is the interface context dependant, working in degraded mode, etc.?

In which way this technology can be qualified of context dependant, transparent, ubiquitous?

Transparency is provided by the fact that in extreme situations medics and paramedics have almost nothing to do: coming close to the victim is enough to trigger the RFID reading of the victim ID (Fig.1). Then the terminal automatically sense the GPS and send the information either to other team members (in case of connection lost to the PC) or to the main server which collate all data from the teams.

Context dependence is provided by the multimodal interface. If the context needs a silent operation, medics or paramedics will only use short messages or written annotation. If they can speak they may prefer to send an audio message to transmit emotional information. At last they can also fill up medical record following a menu based interface.

Ubiquity is provided by a local wireless network that covers the area. In case of disconnection, the network architecture insures security and robustness from a robust data transfer protocol.

We were systemically assessing these properties assessing which functionality was potentially providing the user need.

As an example, if we consider the multimodal interface (Fig. 2 Left), it provides many features of the user need 'context dependence':

- Voice, graphic or text depending of the communication
- Picture or sound to document the situation

Fig. 2. Left : Example of how users can combine several media depending of the context. In this case, the user decided to take a picture of the situation and to make a graphical annotation (a red cross to signal where are the victims). A verbal note has also been monitored to specify the health state of the victims and to make a comment about the situation. Right : Geographical view of the crisis field from the medical point of view. All data pushed in the container are geolocalized on a map with some extra information (e.g. gravity or types of exposure, etc.).

The geographical screen (Fig.2 Right) is providing feature for the user need 'common vision':

- Everybody can have a global view of the situation
- All actors can easily (transparency) document this geographic representation

This approach allowed us to easily check out the completeness of the functional specification. The next step would be to assess it before the prototyping phase.

Simulation to assess the new information technology

We have developed two platforms to assess how this technology can be used in crisis situations. The first one is an agent based platform (Bellamine et al., 2007). It allows simulating large scale scenarios where hundreds of persons are involved. Each actor is represented by an agent. Its activity is procedure based but it has internal states that allow cognitive modeling. The particularity of this simulator is its ability to easily setup depending of the scenario. The output of such simulator can be used to assess both new organizations and technologies (Fig 4, left). The second one is based on a virtual game engine that has been developed for social interaction[1] (El Jed et al. 2006, Dugdale et al., 2006).

---

[1] http://www.irit.fr/~Mehdi.El-Jed/img/these-eljed.pdf

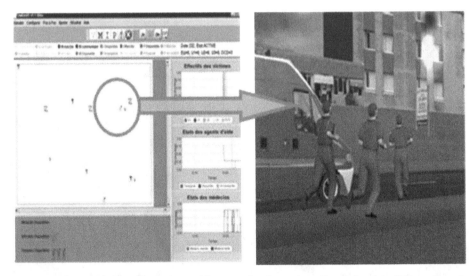

Fig. 3. Left: Screen shot from the multi agent simulator that allows the description of work practices as well as technological constraints. Right: A virtual reality platform allows us to run local scenarios in order to see how users may take advantage of the communication technology they carry with them.

These two simulations are complementary because multi agent models cannot be easily used to represent complex social interactions. Human beings in complex situations may have a highly context dependant behaviour which is difficult to model. In virtual worlds, it is possible to setup enough rich environment and basic social behaviour that allows realistic cooperation.

5 Preliminary Results

At this time this system has been tested both in virtual worlds in a large scale civil simulation involving 50 victims, medics and paramedics. Geolocalisation has been perceived by the stakeholders (firemen and medical team) to be extremely efficient. We observed that officers in charge of the coordination were able to change their plans in real time depending of the situation they were assessing on the centralised map. Field information was almost instantly synthesized at officer's level. Critics were mainly concerning the robustness of the mobile wireless P2P network which was less reliable than a traditional centralized system. From a pragmatic point of view, interoperability between terminals was also a determinant technological choice. In extreme situations, role of actors can change, terminals can be neutralised. In such situations it is mandatory to have a context dependant technology.

6 Conclusion

First results allow us to conclude that the concepts of 'extreme interface' using wireless communication architecture can drastically help first responders in a crisis situation. Several technological characteristics are mandatory:

1) Transparency and ubiquity for the application used by first responders in disaster management or military medics operating in the 'front bubble'. If this constraint is not respected, nobody (as it was observed in the traditional situation) will take time to document the application and feed the officers in charge of the collaboration.
2) The network architecture (like a P2P) should support decentralized collaboration in case where the front teams are no more connected to the central database.
3) Robustness (no data should be lost in case of communication disruption) is a major quality for an emergency system.
4) Spatial coverage is also an important variable. Experts were requesting at least to be able to communicate at the level of a city which means 'few kilometers'. We tested this technology to provide this service but with technologies not available on the shelf (WiMax).

The systemic approach we were using to identify user's needs was not only useful for us in order to specify and to assess our extreme interface concept but it was also a great tool for a participative approach.

References

1. Atkinson, S.R., Moffat, J.: The agile organization. CCRP Publication Series (2005)
2. Bellamine Ben Saoud, N., Ben Mena, T., Dugdale, J., Pavard, B.: Assessing large scale emergency rescue plans: an agent based approach. The International Journal of Intelligent Control and Systems 11(4), 260–271 (2007)
3. Chisholm, D.: Coordination without hierarchy. In: Informal Structures in Multi Organizational Systems, p. 273. University of California Press, Berkeley (1989)
4. Dugdale, J., Pallamin, N., Pavard, B.: An assessment of a mixed reality environment: towards an ethnomethodological approach. Simulation and Gaming 37(2), 1–19 (2006)
5. El Jed, M., Pallamin, N., Pavard, B.: Vers des Communications situées. In: Proceedings of the National Conference on: Coopération, Innovation et Technologie (Cite 2006) June 26, 27 et 28, 2006, Nantes, France (2006)
6. Grote, G.: Rules management as source for loose coupling in high risk systems. In: Proceedings' of ISCRAM 2007, 4th International Conference on Information Systems for Crisis Management, Delft, Netherlands, pp. 537–544 (2007)
7. Harrald, J.R.: Agility and discipline: critical success factors for disaster response. The annals of the American Academy of political and Social Science 604, 256–272 (2006)
8. Jennex, M.E.: Reflections on strong Angel III: some lessons learned. In: Proceeding's of ISCRAM 2007, 4th International Conference on Information Systems for Crisis Management, Delft, Netherlands, pp. 537–544 (2007)
9. Pavard, B., Dugdale, J., Saoud, N., Darcy, S., Salembier, P.: Underlying concepts in robustness and resilience and their use in designing socio-technical systems. In: Resilience Engineering: Remaining sensitive to the possibility of failure, Ashgate (2007)
10. Pavard, B.: User needs analysis for national and international NGO's. Technical Report (GRIC-IRIT - Restricted diffusion) (2007)
11. Steel, K., Pariès, J.: The process of tailoring models for a priori safety and risk management for use within industry. In: Proceedings of Resilience engineering symposium, Mines Paris, pp. 294–124 (2007)

12. Thomson, J.D.: Organizations in action: Social Science Bases of Administrative Theory, p. 13. Mc Graw-Hill, New York (1967)
13. Yang, Z., Rothkrantz, L.J.M.: Emotion sensing for context sensitive interpretation of crisis reports. In: Proceedings' of ISCRAM 2007, 4th International Conference on Information Systems for Crisis Management, Delft, Netherlands, pp. 507–514 (2007)

Supporting Unstructured Activities in Crisis Management: A Collaboration Model and Prototype to Improve Situation Awareness

Cláudio Sapateiro[1], Pedro Antunes[2], Gustavo Zurita[3],
Nelson Baloian[4], and Rodrigo Vogt[3]

[1] Systems and Informatics Department, Superior School of Technology,
Polytechnic Institute of Setúbal, 2914 Setúbal, Portugal
`csapateiro@est.ips.pt`
[2] Department of Informatics, Faculty of Sciences of the University of Lisbon,
Lisbon, Portugal
`paa@di.fc.ul.pt`
[3] Management Control and Information Systems Department, Business School,
Universidad de Chile
`gnzurita@fen.uchile.cl`, `rodrigovogt@gmail.com`
[4] Computer Science Department, Engineering School,
Universidad de Chile
`nbaloian@dcc.uchile.cl`

Abstract. In this paper we explore the construction of Situation Awareness using a collection of mobile, collaborative and visual-interactive devices. These devices provide a shared workspace where multiple users may correlate information about the problematic situation at hand and organize the unstructured activities necessary to handle the situation. A PDA prototype of these mobile, collaborative and visual-interactive devices has already been developed with the purpose to evaluate the feasibility of the collaboration model. The paper describes the collaboration model and presents an application scenario in the emergency management area currently being used to evaluate the prototype.

Keywords: Crisis Management, Unstructured Work Activities, Collaboration, Situation Awareness.

1 Introduction

Organizations orchestrate their work along a continuum of structured and unstructured activities [1, 2], trying to balance quite different and sometimes contradictory criteria such as productivity and responsiveness. Structured activities are designed a priori based on work models addressing coordination issues, productivity, efficiency and consistency. Information Systems (IS) have traditionally been developed with the purpose to automate as much as possible such work models, relieving humans from the coordination effort.

Unfortunately many unknown variables, both external (e.g., market dynamics and natural disasters) and internal (e.g., latent problems, emergent work processes or lack

J. Löffler and M. Klann (Eds.): Mobile Response, LNCS 5424, pp. 101–111, 2009.

of flexibility in work structures), are among the factors that may lead to automation failures and lack of support of existing IS to unstructured work activities occurring when facing unplanned, emergent or highly fluid scenarios. An example of such an unstructured scenario is crisis management. A crisis is an unexpected, unfamiliar chain or combination of events, causing uncertainty of action and time-pressure [3]. In these situations, beyond the scope of work models and contingency plans, people engage in informal relationships and make use of their tacit knowledge in an opportunistic manner. [4] highlights several characteristics of these emergent processes: no best structure or sequence; typically distributed; dynamically evolving; actor roles unpredictable; and unpredictable contexts.

The concept of resilience, which may be characterized as a comprehensive endeavor towards increased resistance and flexibility dealing with crisis situations [5-7], should be a concern of IS development. The purpose is to deploy IS capable to preserve work consistency and effectiveness in unpredicted scenarios extending far beyond the predefined work models.

From an analysis of the proceedings of the International Community on Information Systems for Crisis Response and Management conferences (ISCRAM) between 2004 and 2006, some recurrent concerns in dealing with crisis situations were identified: shared awareness of the situation; information and knowledge representation and management; usability and interface design concerns. [8] and [9] also pointed out that communication, information management and the construction of Situation Awareness (SA) are major issues to consider when addressing crises situations.

Our research aims to study the IS support to unstructured activities based on the collaborative construction of SA. In the next section we present some related work that influenced our approach. In Section Three we present our IS approach to support unstructured work activities. That discussion is continued in Section Four with a description of the developed prototype. Then, in Section Five, we discus a possible application scenario: Emergency Management. Finally, in Section Six we draw some conclusions from our research and point future work directions.

2 Related Work

We may find several projects in the research literature addressing the gap from fully structured activities to ad-hoc unstructured activities, e.g., [2, 10, 11]. These works fundamentally studied how to bring the IS back to model guidance after deviations caused by unpredicted events. The problem addressed by our research goes beyond this perspective towards the support of emergent collaborative work structures, where models do not serve as prescriptions but rather as artifacts that may help getting the work done [12, 13].

Our proposal relies in a constructivist approach to SA. The support to unstructured activities is grounded in the collaborative construction of SA, relying upon the IS to maintain up to date and shared information about the situation.

The most popular definition of SA is from [14], which states that: Situation awareness is the perception of elements in the environment within a volume of time and space, the comprehension of their meaning, and the projection of their status in the near future. This perspective over SA regards perception, comprehension and projection as three essential dimensions.

The support to SA has received considerable attention in the Computer Supported Cooperative Work (CSCW) research field [15-18]. However, the vast majority of this research has focused in specific context/domain proposals, and also in a functional-oriented perspective, while in our research we emphasize a process perspective, considering the resources and activities necessary to obtain, manage and use SA information in crisis scenarios.

Team members should not only be able to monitor and analyze SA, but also anticipate the SA needs of their colleagues. Hence, [19] defines "team SA" as SA plus the mutual adjustment of one and another's minds as they interact as a team in a specific context of action. Rather than considering teams as groups of self-organized people, we should regard them as communities of practice, which encompasses broader issues such as practices, norms and rituals [20].

Designing computational support to the teams' dynamics constitutes a tremendous challenge. We have considered two issues as key design requirements in addressing crisis situations: (1) a minimal work overhead demand; and (2) a rich information visualization schema. [15, 21-23] regard information visualization as a fundamental mean to enhance cognition and information interpretation.

Finally, we should also consider research on contexts of action characterization and representation. Research in this area has been polarized around two main perspectives: positivist and phenomenological [24]. The positivist perspective, which is traditionally adopted by the engineering fields, regards context as a stable information entity and separable from action. In our research we adopt the phenomenological perspective, with strong roots in social sciences, which regards context as a relational entity relating all involved actions and objects, and evolving dynamically as actions unfold [25].

3 Proposed Approach

Our proposed approach to assist emergent work activities consists in a collaboration model supported in a set of shared visual-interactive artifacts named Situation Matrixes (SM). The proposed collaboration model is inspired in several resilience engineering principles [7, 26] emphasizing: redundancy regarding existing IS, power deference among the involved actors, situated action and shared situation awareness. In our approach we aim to enhance the individual contributions to the overall situation understanding and handling. By allowing each involved actor to contribute to situation handling, we promote the externalization of knowledge flows [27], and actors' tacit knowledge and experience. The sharing of individual assessments will also facilitate collective sensemaking [28] and situated framing [13, 29].

For the construction of this shared artifact we adopted a situation characterization framework consisting of a set of Situation Dimensions (SD). Samples of situation dimensions may include: involved actors, required actions, needed resources, events, goals, situational attributes, etc. For a given application domain, an initial set of relevant dimensions may be adopted and later on dynamically redefined, as an unplanned situation unfolds. These dimensions may be completely created and redefined in real time.

The SD are correlated in Situation Matrixes (SM), e.g., Actions versus Actors, Actor versus Allocated Resources, Goals versus Actions, etc. as several SM may be necessary to express complex SD correlations. The SM concept was inspired by the Swiss Cheese model of accidents [30], which posits that for an incident to progress, several organizational layers of defense are crossed trough existing holes, due active or latent failure conditions. Our proposed SM artifact aims to allow the mitigation strategy be composed by the alignment of SD that will prevent the incident from progressing.

The SM may also be defined and organized in layers as the action unfolds.

Our specific implementation of the SM was inspired by the perspective proposed by [31], which uses several types of matrixes to visualize qualitative data, for instance: concept cluster matrixes, empirical matrixes, and temporal or event driven matrixes. In our approach the SD correlations are specified in the SM as circles, using different sizes and/or colors to express the perceived strengths (see Figure 1a). Several alternatives may be considered to express the semantic meaning of such correlations, but in our approach we leave the concrete semantics definition to the experts of the possible application domains.

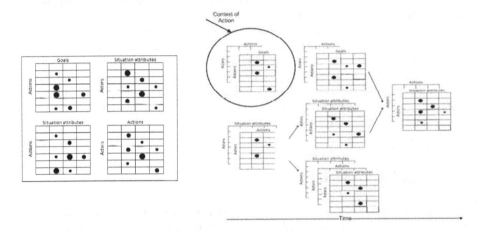

Fig. 1. Situation Matrixes (SM): a) Sample of SM; b) SM evolution

The collection of SM constitutes a shared workspace accomplishing several goals: provide a situation representation shared by the team; support collective and individual action; serve as a monitor/feedback mechanism; and also deliver information in a flexible and manageable way.

As the situation evolves, the SM may include more SD items (e.g., more actors involved, more actions, more situation attributes), with different correlations, and new SM may also be added to the pool (see Figure 1b).

4 Prototype

In this section we present the current status of the prototype development. The prototype supports managing the SM described in the previous section, allowing the collaborative creation, sharing and organization of SD correlations. Since mobility may constitute a key requirement to support emergent work activities, the prototype operates seamlessly with Tablet PC and PDA. Keeping in mind that a minimal overhead is a necessary requirement, the manipulation of SM was designed to be as fast and simple as possible, without limiting the potential to describe and share the different views of the emergent situation that people may have.

The prototype does not support different roles in order to stay as simple and flexible as possible. The prototype operates in a full peer-to-peer model, using the Wi-Fi communication channels available in Tablet PC and PDA. This means that every user has exactly the same application and seamlessly interacts with every other user running the application in the vicinity.

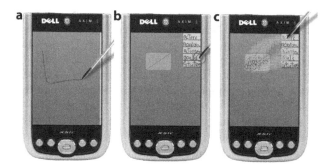

Fig. 2. PDA prototype: a) SM creation; b) SD selection; c) SM composition

The prototype was developed on top of a pen-based application framework developed at the University of Chile. Besides handling all communication and collaboration issues, this framework provides a very rich collection of predefined pen-based gestures supporting the creation and manipulation of visual objects [32].

Concerning the way users interact with the prototype, a new SM is defined by drawing half a rectangle (see Figure 2a). The user assigns the respective SD to each side of the rectangle (Figure 2b-c). Double-clicking a SM it will open the matrix and by double-clicking the sides of the matrix affords creating rows and columns (Figures 3a-c). Handwritten text is used to specify both SD and rows and columns headers, although there is also the possibility to select predefined ones from a menu. Finally, the correlations in the matrix are defined with double-clicking gestures (Figure 3d).

When the size of the rectangle becomes larger, it may be navigated with left-right and up-down gestures. There are also available zoom-in and zoom-out gestures to navigate within the rectangle.

Fig. 3. Managing the SM: a) b) column insertion; c) row insertion; d) specifying correlations

Currently, the navigation between several SM must be accomplished by selecting the small rectangle at the top-left corner, which leads the user to a workspace displaying all available SM. Please note that although the SM are shared, the users individually interact with the workspace, i.e. there are no tightly coupling.

A final note regarding the prototype, to refer that when a connection is not possible users may update their SM when in the proximity of other user and exchange SM between them by an Ir link. A compability mode is available to deal with the differences.

5 Application Scenario

When facing an emergency situation two main behaviors will coexist: rule-based behavior and knowledge-based behavior. Rule based behavior relies on existing contingency plans originated from simulations and training. On the other hand, knowledge-based behavior relies on contextual information, tacit knowledge and expertise to address contingencial factors. The developed approach addresses the support of team collaboration aiming to improve actions consistency when dealing with such unplanned factors.

[33] showed that several emergency scenarios (e.g., fires, floods) share common crisis management characteristics, such as: teams organization, information paths, cross teams communication and information needs. For instance, a common firefighter's organization is based on the Incident Commander (IC), as an organizer and decision-maker. Depending on the size of the situation, the operations are conducted in the field by several companies, each one constituted by a Captain and a small group of firefighters.

The major requirements to collaboration between the IC and the Captains were identified by [34]:

- Accountability: Accountability of resources and personnel.
- Assessment: Assessment of the situation through multiple sources.
- Awareness: Promoting a shared awareness of the situation.
- Communication: Communication support should add reliability and/or redundancy to existing channels.

Actually IC and Captains maintain situation awareness by communicating through radio and/or meeting face-to-face at regular intervals. However, this type of collaboration lacks information persistency [35]. With the proposed approach beside the support of information persistency, by allowing involved actors to monitor and participate in a shared workspace, the system will also provide a valuable feedback mechanism of operational status. As the emergency situation unfolds, the situational dimensions (involved actors, needed resources, proposed actions, etc.) may also evolve. The correlations between these dimensions will be continuously updated, according to different perspectives coming from the field. This perspective is supported in several interviews and ethnographic studies analysis, developed by us and a number of authors e.g. [35, 36].

This approach can be extended to the support of cross-organizational collaborations, e.g., between Police, Civil Protection and Firefighters, which often face communication barriers. For instance, the different forces in Portugal use non-compatible radio communications devices and sometimes the IC has to listen to three radios plus a cellular phone. The shared workspace affords bringing together scattered information. It is however expected that some training and discipline be necessary to develop social protocols and to devise the best ways to organize this information coming from several people in the field as also presented in [3, 37]. The prototype purposefully does not control who is allowed to modify the SD and SM, thus allowing the level of flexibility envisaged by the notion of resilience.

Next, we present a description of the proposed model and prototype usage by firefighters in an emergency situation. Since IC usually stays at a safe distance of the incident (but close enough to be aware) he/she could be equipped with a tablet PC (Figure 4) which due the dimension and interface may promote a better overall situation state awareness and application usability, and deliver to company captains PDAs which will assist them in the management of relevant awareness information to their context of action and also in their contributions to the solution strategy.

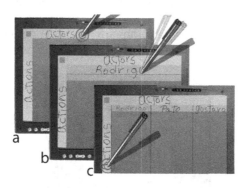

Fig. 4. Managing the SM – Tablet PC: a) b) column insertion; c) row insertion

5.1 Prototype Usage Description

After an alarm is received, depending on the perceived scale of the accident, a predetermined number of emergency response resources are dispatched. On the way to the incident location teams receive by radio additional information regarding the type of incident they will face (e.g. a urban fire), such as weather conditions, existence of victims, existence of dangerous materials in the neighborhood, …

Once identified the type of incident a set of initial (pre-determined) SM can be selected containing typical dimensions necessary to address the kind of situation (in this example they could be for instance Situational Attributes versus Actions, Situational Attributes versus Actors and Actors versus Actions). The situational attributes presented above (weather conditions, existence of victims, existence of dangerous materials) could be registered in a Situation Attributes dimension and related with other dimensions such as Actions to take (e.g. to deal with the presence of dangerous materials), and/or involved Actors (e.g. with specific expertise for dealing with dangerous materials). All the situation dimensions, could initially contain typical items, for instance, the Actions dimension could enumerate typical actions under the type of faced scenario: crowd control, traffic control, obtain fire hydrants locations, etc. Also recommended correlations (e.g. expert actor to specific action) could already exist in the SM cells.

Usually the highest rank of the first team that arrives to incident location will assume the IC role. This team will make a quick in place size-up of the situation considering an initial assessment of: hazards, safety procedures, incident scope, etc. and develop an attack plan. Again, regarding the situation assessment a set of SM can be selected (or created) to accommodate information gathered. If the situation demands, more resources are requested and the IC role may be passed to a higher rank that arrives later on, providing a quick status report. Since information is persisted in a set of SM, they may help this role transition in a very important issue: perceive overall situation status.

As situation evolves, a problematic concern for IC is to track resources allocation, "who or what is where and doing what?" (accountability and awareness above presented requirements [34]). Usually, IC has a number of threads going on and information comes from multiple sources. To overcome this problem the set of SM: Resources versus Actors, Actors versus Locations, Resources versus Actions and Resources versus Locations could be used. Figure 5 shows SM relating resources with respective responsible actors, being operated in a PDA.

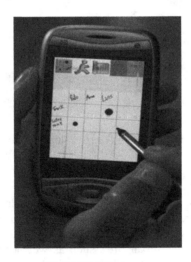

Fig. 5. PDA Prototype

A *locations* dimension may be important if an incident is large enough, because in such cases, companies will be organized into divisions which operate within a specific geographic region (e.g. north, third floor). Divisions may also be organized in groups which perform specific functions (e.g. rescue, medical care).

Since, with this approach, a lot of incident's related information is registered, the proposed prototype has an additional utility: it will allow a posteriori analysis of the course of action to promote further improvement in procedures, as well as new situation dimensions (and respective dimension items) and/or SMs to be initially available for future occurrences.

6 Discussion and Future Work

In this paper we describe a collaboration model and prototype aiming to support the unstructured activities that emerge in emergency scenarios due to contingential factors. The adoption of our prototype assumes that agents involved in these scenarios are professionals with expertise in emergency management and have specific training. In this way the information shared through the prototype will have a clear meaning to the involved actors.

We should note that similar collaborative approaches exist and are already used in some other domains. For instance, flight operators and firefighters adopted several variations/generations of the Crew Resource Management (CRM) training, which has its foundations concerning not so much the technical knowledge and required skills but rather the interpersonal skills used for gaining and maintaining situation awareness, solving problems and making decisions [38, 39]. The CRM approaches fosters a climate and a culture where the freedom to respectfully question authority is encouraged, aiming to increase resilience while reducing the discrepancy between what is happening and what should be happening.

Keeping the IS up to date in these scenarios, without adding unacceptable overheads, presents major challenges to IS developers. For instance, status reports and situation assessments are hard to track due to dependencies on the explicit user interactions and information volatility.

We have been studying a pulling strategy to IS support in this context: as information becomes old, the users may be prompted to report on their validity, in combination with a visualization schema to express the degradation of the quality of the available information. For now we are considering two ways to implement such concept: 1- when users input information, a deadline is also introduced (e.g. valid for the next 15 min); 2- if no deadline is introduced that correlation will incrementally became more transparent as time goes by. Once we refine the prototype, a field evaluation should be made. The preliminary step of our evaluation methodology will be to conduct a workshop with domain experts and discuss the proposed approach in a scenario based evaluation.

Acknowledgements

The research supporting this work was partially financed by Portuguese FCT Project POSI/EIA/57038/2004 and Chile - Fondecyt Project Nr. 1085010.

References

1. Sheth, A., et al.: Workflow and process automation in Information Systems. In: NSF Workshop (1996)
2. Bernstein, A.: How can cooperative work tools support dynamic group processes? Bridging the specifity frontier. In: CSCW (2000)
3. ESSAY. Enhanced Safety through Situation Awareness Integration in training. European Community ESSAY project: Contract No GRD1-1999-10450 (2000)

4. Markus, M.L., Majchrzak, A., Gasser, L.: A design theory for systems that support emergent knowledge processes. MIS Quaterly (2002)
5. Cocchiara, R.: Beyond disaster recovery: becoming a resiliente business. IBM whitepaper (2007)
6. Sheffi, Y.: Building a resilient organization. MIT, Cambridge (2006)
7. Hollnagel, E., Woods, D.D.: Resilience Engineering Precepts. A. Publishing (2006)
8. Milis, K., Walle, B.V.d.: IT for Corporate Crisis Management: Findings from a Survey in 6 different Industries on Management Attention, Intention and Actual Use. In: ISCRAM (2007)
9. Kanno, T., Futura, K.: Resilience of emergency response systems (2006)
10. Dourish, P., et al.: Freeflow: Mediating between representation and action in workflow systems. In: CSCW, USA (1996)
11. Mourão, H., Antunes, P.: Supporting effective unexpected exceptions handling in workflow management systems. In: SAC, Seoul, korea (2007)
12. Suchman, L.: Plans and Situated Actions: The problem of human-machine communication. Cambridge University Press, Cambridge (1987)
13. Gasson, S.: A social action model of situated information systems design. The Data Base for Advances in Information Systems 30(2) (1999)
14. Endsley, M.: Toward a theory of situation awareness in dynamic systems. Human Factors 37(1), 32–64 (1995)
15. Storey, M.-A.D., Cubranic, D., German, D.: On the Use of Visualization to Support Awareness of Human Activities in Software Development: A Survey and a Framework (2004)
16. Neale, D.C., Carroll, J.M., Rosson, M.B.: Evaluating Computer-Supported cooperative work: Models and frameworks. In: CSCW (2004)
17. Gutwin, C., Greenberg, S.: A descriptive framework of workspace awareness for real time groupware. In: CSCW (November 2002)
18. Bolstad, C.A., Endsley, M.R.: Shared displays and team performance. In: Human Performance, Situation Awareness and Automation (2000)
19. Shu, Y., Futura, K.: An inference method of team situation awareness based on mutual awareness. Cognition, Technology & Work 7, 272–287 (2005)
20. Garrety, K., Robertson, P.L., Badham, R.: Communities of Pratice, actor networks and learning in development projects. In: The Future of Innovation Studies, 2001. ECIS, Netherlands (2001)
21. Donath, J.S.: Visual Who: Animating activities of an electronic community. ACM Multimedia, California (1995)
22. Erickson, T., et al.: A Social Proxy for Distributed Tasks: Design and Evaluation of a Working Prototype. In: CHI 2004, Vienna, Austria (2004)
23. Thomas, J.J., Cook, K.A.: Illuminating the Path. NVAC (2004)
24. Dourish, P.: What we talk about when we talk about context. Personal and Ubiquitous Computing (2004)
25. Borges, M.R.S., et al.: Groupware system design the context concept. In: Shen, W.-m., Lin, Z., Barthès, J.-P.A., Li, T.-Q. (eds.) CSCWD 2004. LNCS, vol. 3168, pp. 45–54. Springer, Heidelberg (2005)
26. McManus, S., et al.: Resilience Management: A framework for Assessing and Improving the resilience of organizations (2007), http://www.resorgs.org.nz/
27. Nonaka, I., Takeuchi, H.: The knowledge-creating company. Oxford University Press, Oxford (1995)
28. Weick, K.E.: Sense Making in Organizations. Sage Publications, Thousand Oaks (1996)

29. Gasson, S.: A Framework For Behavioral Studies of Social Cognitio. In: Information Systems. ISOneWorld (2004)
30. Reason, J.T.: Managing the risks of organizational accidents. Ashgate, Aldershot (1997)
31. Miles, M.B., Huberman, A.M.: Qualitative data analysis. Sage Publications, Thousand Oaks (1994)
32. Zurita, G., et al.: Using PDAs in meetings: Patterns, Architecture and Components. Journal of Universal Computer Science 14(1) (2008) (Special Issue on Groupware: Issues and applications)
33. Berrouard, D., Cziner, K., Boukalov, A.: Emergency Scenario User Perspective in Public Safety Communication Systems. In: ISCRAM (2006)
34. Jiang, X., et al.: Ubiquitous computing for firefighters: Field studies and prototypes of large displays for incident comand. In: CHI (2004)
35. Landgren, J.: Designing Information Technology for Emergency Response, Department of applied Information Technology. Goteborg University, Goteborg (2007)
36. Landgren, J.: Making action visible in time critical work. In: CHI Proceedings (2006)
37. Wybo, J.-L., Latiers, M.: Exploring complex emergency situations' dynamic: theoretical, epistemological and methodological proposals. Int. J. Emergency Management 3(1), 40–51 (2006)
38. Helmereich, R.L., Merrit, A.C., Wilhelm, J.A.: The evlution of Crew Resource managemnt Training in commercial Aviation. International Journal of Aviation Psychology 9(1), 19–32 (1999)
39. Tippet, J.: Crew Resource Management Manual - A positive change for the fire service. I.A.o.F. Chiefs. (2002), http://www.iafc.org/

Ontology-Based Rescue Operation Management

Stasinos Konstantopoulos[1], Jens Pottebaum[2], Jochen Schon[3],
Daniel Schneider[3], Thomas Winkler[3], Georgios Paliouras[1], and Rainer Koch[2]

[1] Institute of Informatics and Telecommunications,
NCSR 'Demokritos', Ag. Paraskevi 153 10, Athens, Greece
{konstant,paliourg}@iit.demokritos.gr
[2] Unversity of Paderborn, C.I.K., Pohlweg 47-49, 33098 Paderborn
{pottebaum,r.koch}@cik.uni-paderborn.de
[3] Fraunhofer IAIS, Schloss Birlinghoven, Sankt Augustin, Germany
{jochen.schon,daniel.schneider,thomas.winkler}@iais.fraunhofer.de

Abstract. The focus of this paper is ontology-based knowledge management in the framework of a mobile communication and information system for rescue operation management. We present a novel ontology data service, combining prior domain knowledge about large-scale rescue operations with dynamic information about a developing operation. We also discuss the integration of such a data service into a service-oriented application framework to reach high performance and accessibility, and offer examples of SHARE applications to demonstrate the practical benefits of the approach chosen.

1 Introduction: The Fire Fighting Domain

Mobile information technology is a key technology in the emergency-response domain, as emergency forces deployed at a disaster site have very limited access to conventional IT infrastructure. Currently, IT is limited to operation control centres in the fire stations and even IT-based emergency dispatch systems are, typically, not linked to other information systems.

As a result, on-site operation management is conducted over paper maps, magnetic boards, analogue radio, hand-written message forms, and fax. Especially for large-scale operations these tools are often not sufficient for the complex emergency management task at hand. As a result, commands processed via hand-written message forms might, in multi-level command hierarchy operations, need as much as 20 minutes to reach their destination, and staff personnel involved in decision-making lacks a comprehensive, integrated view of the various aspects of the operation.

By contrast, mobile information technology can be a valuable tool in the hands of emergency professionals to increase speed, precision, efficiency and effectiveness of their operations. Mobile IT, however, has to overcome immense entry barriers prior to its widespread use in the rescue-operation domain; most importantly immaturity and instability of the technology, higher cost of equipment, and the heterogeneity of the organizational structure of SaR departments.

J. Löffler and M. Klann (Eds.): Mobile Response, LNCS 5424, pp. 112–121, 2009.

The gap between the great benefit that usable mobile IT could yield in the domain of emergency response and the specific challenges for such technologies in this particularly demanding domain, results in a situation which calls for a new strategy to release this immense potential with a sustainable impact. The FP6-IST SHARE project[1] carried out extensive research and development work in the domain, and proposed introducing a few small but extremely efficient solutions that substantially help rescue units, instead of building an overall solution that is meant to replace all existing tools at once. Another important step towards usability and robustness was the introduction of semantic representation technology to support a number of SHARE end-user applications.

The rest of this paper is organized as follows: we first provide an overview of the SHARE system (Section 2) and then describe SHARE-ODS, its central knowledge representation and management component (Section 3). We proceed to present some key SHARE applications and discuss how they capitalize on SHARE-ODS (Section 4), and finally conclude (Section 5).

2   A Mobile Information and Communication System

The SHARE system is a service-oriented application framework, supporting management tasks in large-scale rescue operations. The main applications available to rescue team members cover the following functionalities: interactive operation map (MAP), Push-to-Share communications (PTS), digital message forms (DMF), interactive resource management (IRM) and, finally, communications indexing and retrieval. Multimodal interfaces using automatic speech recognition and text-to-speech synthesis are available for most of the applications to enable hands-free access to the services offered. Figure 1 shows the graphical user interfaces of the applications. Depending on the task (strategical, tactical, operational) the appropriate application is selected by the users; depending on the user's operational role, different functionality is provided by each application, matching the role's responsibilities and access rights.

Although fire brigade personnel are highly motivated with respect to using new technologies, working with new and complex IT-based systems while heavily involved in an operation is poses extra difficulties. With this in mind, we identified the applications that are in the centre of operation management and that show a great potential as entry points for mobile IT into the domain. The two main applications we identified are the digital operation map on the one hand and the interactive resource management on the other.

Domain knowledge about rescue operations is logically represented as an ontology and accessed during the operation via an ontology data service. The main advantages of interlinking SHARE applications by an ontological knowledge base will be described in the following sections. Logical inference is mostly used in resource planning and decision making. The dynamic characteristics of ontology-based knowledge management allow a flexible configuration of group-based

---

[1] See also http://www.ist-share.org/

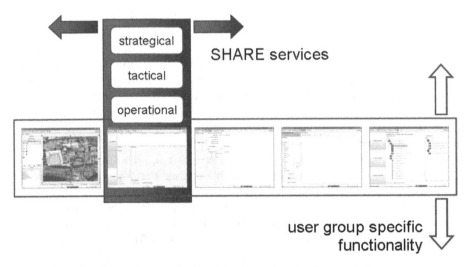

Fig. 1. Usage of SHARE applications in the operation

communication. Finally, robust indexing and retrieval of multimedia communication messages benefit from the usage of an ontology in the SHARE system.

3   Knowledge Management in SHARE

The knowledge management system relies on Semantic Web technologies in order to model the operation, derive inferences from the model, and provide for the interaction between the (inferred) model and the end-user operation management applications. More specifically, the operation is modelled as an *ontology*, an abstract representation often used in the areas of knowledge representation, artificial intelligence and the Semantic Web as a way of structuring and representing knowledge.

3.1   Conceptual View: Ontology Structure

The elementary pieces of information in the ontology – corresponding to the individuals of the domain of discourse – are called *instances*. In the SHARE Ontology, instances correspond to officers, vehicles, units, audio and video documents exchanged, geographical sections of the operation, and so on. These instances are organized in a conceptual hierarchy where each *concept* or *class* groups together a set of conceptually similar instances.

The SHARE conceptual model comprises two main hierarchies, one involving concepts from the search-and-rescue domain and one involving multimedia objects. In addition, there are auxiliary concepts represents spatio-temporal references.

SaRThing is the top concept of the search-and-rescue hierarchy and subsumes concepts such as: Formation, OperationalRole, Personnel, Equipment, Vehicle, Station, etc. Formation, OperationalRole, and Personnel, in particular, are further specialized into A, B, and C-Level, to reflect the three-level operational structure followed in fire brigade operations. MultimediaThing, on the other hand, subsumes logical representations of the metadata of all documents (DMF, audio, and video) generated and transmitted during an operation.

Personnel instances are not directly related to Formation instances, but only an OperationalRole instance which specifies the each officer's role in the operation. This approach allows modelling multiple roles being assigned to the same person, as is, for example, the case with A-Level staff members in smaller operations.

Both main sub-ontologies as well as the auxiliary ones are tightly integrated in a comprehensive model of the operation and extensively cross-linked using ontological *relations* between their instances. Some of the most prominent relations are partOf relations, which link Formation instances into a command structure and Section and Subsection geo-reference instances into a geographical decomposition of the various tasks and sub-tasks carried out. It should be noted that the geographical structure does not necessarily match the operational one: for instance, a supply or rescue-service formation might be assigned a section (area of responsibility) which overlaps with several fire-fighting formations' sections.

3.2   Logical View: Ontological Reasoning

The SHARE Ontology is represented in OWL-DL [1], a web semantics representation language that is compatible with Description Logics (DL). DLs are a family of formal logics falling inside a *decidable* fragment of first-order predicate logic. The $\mathcal{SHOIN}$ description logic is of particular interest, as it is the minimal DL that covers OWL-DL [2].

DL reasoners, like Pellet[2] used in SHARE, are used to deduce knowledge that is implicit in the model, based on explicit facts and axioms present in the ontology. In SHARE, for example, the A, B, and C-Level Formation concepts are refined into sub-concepts which include *well-formed* formations at each alarm level. Fire brigade rules and practices with respect to operational structure are represented as axioms concerning membership in the well-formed sub-class of each formation class. So, for instance, for alarm level 4 we have provided the following axioms:

$$ALF4 \equiv \quad ALevelForm \sqcap \forall hasProSub.BLF4 \sqcap\ \geq 2\ hasProSub \sqcap\ \leq 2\ hasProSub \sqcap$$
$$\forall hasResSub.MANV2 \sqcap\ \geq 1\ hasResSub \sqcap\ \leq 1\ hasResSub$$
$$BLF4 \equiv \quad BLevelForm \sqcap \forall hasProSub.CLF4 \sqcap\ \geq 2\ hasProSub \sqcap\ \leq 2\ hasProSub$$
$$CLF4 \equiv \quad CLevelForm \sqcap\ \geq 3\ hasVehicle \sqcap\ \leq 5\ hasVehicle$$

to represent the following rules about alarm level 4 operations: the A-Level Formation must have exactly 2 professional fire brigade B-Levels and 1 MANV2 rescue formation. The two B-Level Formations must have 2 full C-Level Formations, which have 3 to 5 vehicles each.

Given these axioms, an operation's compliance with alarm level 4 guidelines is checked by logically verifying that all Formation instances of the operation are

---

[2] See http://pellet.owldl.com/ for more information.

subsumed under ALF4, BLF4, or CLF4, depending on the formation level they belong to. Compliance with the rest of the alarm levels is checked in a similar fashion.

3.3   Technical View: Embedding the Ontology

One of the main concerns while designing the system architecture was how to make the knowledge, stored in the ontology, available and useful to the client applications. By analysing the requirements of those applications towards the knowledge base it was possible to identify a set of hierarchically structured services called SHARE-ODS.

3.3.1   Hierarchical Service Structure

The SHARE Ontology Data Service [3], is a set of comprehensive data and knowledge services for the SHARE system. It provides access to the ontology and the reasoner's conclusions through web services, presenting a specifically customized API populating, updating, and querying the SHARE knowledge base to each client application. SHARE-ODS provides additional extra-logical functionality, like logging and client-specific composite functionality. Composite functionality groups together commonly-recurring service calls into a single call, providing a high-level interface to the ontology.

A high-level API might not only add, but also restrict functionality by blocking access to low-level functions. For instance, the API presented to the retrieval application permits querying about document meta-data and related operational structure, but does not permit updating the knowledge base. The PTS API, on the other hand, provides a method for adding new audio and video documents and for relating them to SaR instances, but does not permit the addition of new units; structural changes in the operation (commiting and relieving units, moving units around) can only be performed thought the IRM API, and so on.

This also provides limited access-rights management capabilities, by presenting to each client an API which offers only functionality matching the access rights allocated to the user of the client application. In order that a fire officer can use the client application he has to be assigned a functional role within the regular workflow of the operation. Starting the client application the officer is authenticated by the SHARE system; the person is matched to the role assignments. Each role may execute a different set of applications, affecting (a) the available top level use cases, (b) the information displayed and (c) the functionalities and their options. Actions out of a role's responsibility are not available as application options, and the officer filling the role has to request such actions following the chain of command.

3.3.2   Synchronization of Critical Information

In the course of an operation, new facts about the operation and its various agents get added to the SHARE-ODS knowledge base. Some of this information is critical as it has a direct impact on the system configuration or need to be reacted upon immediately. Examples for this kind of information are changes in the communication group structure or updates of the operation map.

The challenge in this context is efficiently and timely notifying client applications that they need to synchronize their internal information structures with the ODS. In the first SHARE prototype this was approached with *polling* in fixed time intervals. This approach proved sub-optimal, as short intervals were very resource demanding and had a negative impact on the overall response time of the system. Longer intervals, on the other hand, did not honour the time critical nature of the information.

This was addressed by replacing polling with a synchronization mechanism based on the *Java Message Service* (JMS). JMS provides for *topics*, thematically separated messaging systems, where JMS clients participate as subscribers, publishers, or both. In SHARE, topics correspond to client applications (i.e. MAP-Topic, IRM-Topic a.s.o) that potentially need to react to the update. Any application that updates the knowledge base will subsequently send message to the appropriate topic, so that subscribed clients know to contact SHARE-ODS to also update their internal information structures. Following this approach information is timely updated without any noticeable delays in the system response time.

4 Ontology-Driven Services

Several services in SHARE interact with the ontology via the SHARE-ODS. Generally, these services provide the ontology with information gained from user input or extracted from media data, and vice versa request collected and derived data from the ontology. Hence, the decision support, the group-based communication and the media indexing and retrieval described in this section are enabled or enhanced by some means or another using the SHARE Ontology.

4.1 Decision Support for Resource Management

In the field of emergency response, resource management tasks are critical to the efficiency of an operation: commanders base their decisions on the availability of resources, the operational and geographical situation, and the various regulations and practices governing fire-brigade operations. These three aspects must correspond to each other, thus the hierarchy of the command must be congruent to the geography of the operations theatre and in accordance to fire-brigade rules.

The most important resources are personnel and vehicles, which might arrive at the operation site already organized into small units or might be allocated to units on-site. At the time of their arrival, they are available, but *non-operative* resources. Before being deployed, units might be organized into larger B or C-level formations, in which case they are *prepared resources*. To become *operative*, non-operative, loose units might be allocated to existing formations, or prepared formations might be wholesome deployed.

Especially for larger operations, this involves a complex coordination job where formations are organized, assigned a commanding officer, assistants and staff, and integrated into the command and communication structure. The coordination of this structure is the foundation of the documentation of an operation and an important instrument concerning fire-brigade regulations. The fundamental use cases for a resource management tool is to view and manage personnel, vehicles, and other equipment available on-site and support starting, escalating, de-escalating, and terminating fire brigade operations, relieving and replacing units or formations, and re-allocating resources; all abiding by the established command structure patterns permitted by the current alarm level (cf. Section 3).

Interactive Resource Management (IRM) [4] is one of the most important functionalities of the SHARE system, presenting resources to the A-level staff in an intuitive and usable way and supporting them in:

- command & control, offering comprehensive and cross-indexed information about the operation;
- visualizing the operation through tactical symbols on a digital map, including annotations about available resources and cross-referencing geographical and operational items;
- quickly and easily retrieving past communications.

Furthermore, of great benefit is information derived from the relations between the various decision-support tools: different applications can update each other and refer to a consistent knowledge base, complementary data pools help build more complete view, and implicit information can be logically inferred from explicit facts. Fire-brigade practices regarding operation structuring and resource allocation and utilization can be easily implemented (cf. Section 3.2 above) and the interplay between geo-references and resource-based structural relations more easily managed [5].

4.2 Dynamic Configuration of Group-Based Communication

One of the core components of the SHARE system is the *push-to-share* (PTS) voice and video communication system. PTS replaces currently-used radio devices which are limited to broadcasting with a group-based communications system, where audio and video messages are only received by automatically-inferred recipients. This functionality is an imperative requirement for emergency operations, as it retains the simplicity of push-to-talk while at the same reducing the clutter of irrelevant messages caused by radio broadcasting.

The PTS system establishes communication groups according to the command-and-communications structure of the operation. At the beginning of an operation, the IRM tool is used to setup the initial command structure and assign units and personnel to formations. SHARE-ODS infers the communication groups from the command structure and logical rules modelling actual fire brigade communication practices. PTS devices query SHARE-ODS for communication group membership information, completing the initial configuration.

Changes in the command structure during the operation (unit or personnel re-allocations, operation escalation or de-escalation, etc.) are also performed through the IRM application. SHARE-ODS re-calculates communication groups to comply with the new command structure, and the PTS system is accordingly re-configured. IRM messages the PTS clients which are directly or indirectly connected to those changes, i.e., are in the same communication group, and the PTS system is reconfigured. Ongoing voice conferences at the time of the update are, naturally, preserved regardless of whether the relevant communication group exits in the new configuration.

4.3   Robust Media Indexing and Retrieval

Retrieval of voice and text communications is a necessary functionality during a rescue operation, but also important for later analysis of large-scale operations or training events. While querying DMF archives is straightforward, automatic speech recognition (ASR) techniques are needed to spot and index keywords in the voice communications. Rescue operations, however, cover very diverse acoustic environments, with a wide range of noise of varying in type and level; a challenging environment which significantly decreases the performance of ASR.

In SHARE, indexing relies on detecting keywords in unconstrained speech, based on a holistic statistical paradigm integrating various knowledge sources such as acoustic, language and pronunciation models. A phoneme-based garbage model [6] is used to detect a set of keywords after applying Wiener Filtering to reduce noise. Training is performed on domain-specific speech data collected during exercises of the Dortmund fire brigade. Acoustic models have been adapted to the commanding tone of the fire fighters, local accent, and the transmission characteristics of the headsets used in SHARE [7].

To further improve the accuracy of the recogniser and increase the robustness of the indexing, minimizing the vocabulary of the ASR is of paramount importance. SHARE-ODS supports ASR by predicting a vocabulary which is as small as possible without lacking important keywords, based on the hierarchical command structure of the operation. This list includes vehicle radio names, personnel names and roles, section codes, and street names that are relevant to the operation. As a rescue operation is a dynamic process, operating units and their subordination as well as responsibilities for sections and streets might change continuously, hence the keyword list for each PTS device user will be dynamic.

SHARE-ODS infers the abstract SARThing instances (operational roles, formations, units, etc.) that are pertinent each PTS communication session, based on operation-structural relations between the members of the session and the rest of the operation. PTSSessions instances are related to the inferred SARThing instances at the time of addition of each PTSSessions to the ontology; in this manner these relevance relations persist subsequent structural changes in the operation, so that SHARE-ODS provides a keyword list which reflects the status of the operation at the time when the PTS session took place.

This list of keywords is finally merged with a small static list of user independent, generic keywords and relevant geographical keywords (street and place names) extracted from the map application. The combined list is used as vocabulary for the ASR module, significantly improving keyword spotting results.

Using one uniform keyword list for all possible commanding units would require a list of several thousand words, as all possible street names, personnel names, vehicle radio names, and section specifiers would have to be covered.

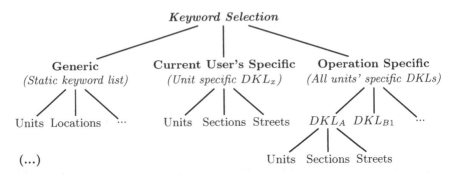

Fig. 2. Example for clustering keywords for a guided keyword selection

Generally, it is easy to see that the number of words in a shared static keyword list will be larger than the number of words in the dynamically-created keyword lists used in SHARE.

SHARE-ODS dynamic keyword lists are also used to provide user-specific clustering and selection for information retrieval. Queries for keywords in a voice communication can be formulated in several ways: a single keyword can be chosen from a list or typed directly into the query field; but also groups or subgroups of keywords—e.g. *all units* and *all sections* or the units and the sections subordinated to a specified user—can be selected. In this latter case, dynamic keyword lists provide a intuitive selection of keyword sets that are very likely to match a user's intentions.

In Figure 2 an example of a hierarchical keyword structure is presented, guiding the user to groups and subgroups of keywords. Generic keywords and specific (dynamic) keywords for the current user are the main clusters. For higher commanding levels and for operation and training analysis it is also possible to access the dynamic keyword lists of all involved commanding units.

The dynamic keyword list for each unit is managed and updated by the ontology. The ontology regularly provides each client application with the update of all dynamic keyword lists which can be selected for a query. So it is assured that every keyword which has been used for indexing during the operation can also be used for retrieval.

5   Conclusions

In this paper we discussed SHARE, a powerful platform, integrating communication and information services to support large-scale rescue operations. After introducing the domain and its challenges, we discussed the SHARE ontology data service (ODS) and.

We have also shown how SHARE-ODS acts as the central information and knowledge management for SHARE, extending the explicitly stored information and allowing the seamless coupling of a variety of heterogeneous applications. This coupling provided the basis for new features, but also allowed for the modular design of SHARE, which we have argued to be an important factor for the introduction of IT technologies in the mobile response domain.

To demonstrate the above, we have presented three SHARE applications (resource management, communications, and multimedia indexing/retrieval) and discussed the considerable benefits of SHARE-ODS support, a discussion further supported by the evaluation of the SHARE system at Dortmund Fire Brigade exercises.

References

1. Smith, M.K., Welty, C., McGuinness, D.L.: OWL web ontology language. Technical report, World Wide Web Consortium, W3C Recommendation (2004), http://www.w3.org/TR/owl-guide/
2. Horrocks, I., Patel-Schneider, P.F., van Harmelen, F.: From SHIQ and RDF to OWL: The making of a web ontology language. Journal of Web Semantics 1(1), 7–26 (2003)
3. Konstantopoulos, S., Paliouras, G., Chatzinotas, S.: SHARE-ODS: an ontology data service for search and rescue operations. In: Antoniou, G., Potamias, G., Spyropoulos, C., Plexousakis, D. (eds.) SETN 2006. LNCS, vol. 3955, pp. 525–528. Springer, Heidelberg (2006)
4. Pottebaum, J., Konstantopoulos, S., Koch, R., Paliouras, G.: SaR resource management based on Description Logics. In: Löffler, J., Klann, M. (eds.) Mobile Response 2007. LNCS, vol. 4458, pp. 61–70. Springer, Heidelberg (2007)
5. Löffler, J., Schon, J., Hernandez-Ernst, V., Pottebaum, J., Koch, R.: Intelligent use of geospatial information for emergency operation management. In: van der Walle, B., Burghardt, P., Nieuwenhuis, K. (eds.) Proceedings of the fourth international conference on information systems for crisis management, ISCRAM 2007, Brussels. Academic and Scientific Publishers, NV (2007)
6. Wilpon, J.G., Rabiner, L.R., Lee, C.H., Goldman, E.R.: Automatic recognition of keywords in unconstrained speech using HMMs. IEEE Transactions on Acoustics, Speech and Signal Processing 38, 1870–1878 (1990)
7. Schneider, D., Winkler, T., Löffler, J., Schon, J.: Robust audio indexing and keyword retrieval optimized for the rescue operation domain. In: Löffler, J., Klann, M. (eds.) Mobile Response 2007. LNCS, vol. 4458, pp. 135–142. Springer, Heidelberg (2007)

Critical Lessons Learned: Evaluation of Commercial Mobile Incident Support Systems

Jonas Landgren

Viktoria Insitute, Public Safety Research Group, Hörselgången 4,
417 56 Göteborg, Sweden
jonas.landgren@viktoria.se

Abstract. This paper reports from a study of two projects concerning the evaluation of commercial mobile incident support systems. Based on data from ethnographic fieldwork and field experiments, key issues and critical lessons learned from these projects are outlined.

Keywords: Emergency response, human-computer interaction, evaluation.

1 Introduction

Mobile information technology has in the last few years become a key issue in emergency response work. Many organizations are running initiatives that will result in the introduction of such technology for field operative personnel. The accumulation of more and more information technology at the operational level in emergency response work [7] is not new. But up until now, mobile information technology has not been affordable to be deployed on a wide scale in emergency response organizations. A specific category of information technology for emergency response is mobile incident support systems. Such systems are designed to target the needs and use of the commander of the fire crew.

This paper reports from two projects where local fire and rescue services have tested and evaluated commercial mobile incident support systems. The paper outlines critical lessons learned.

2 Related Work

This paper follows previous research on user-centered design where the user and the contextual aspects of the work setting are understood as critical.

A study of mobile, in-vehicle information technology for police officers illustrates the complexity of introducing information technology that improves collaboration between dispatchers and police officers, while at the same time conforms to the contextual demands of the field operative. The lack of focus on the actual users during the development resulted in a system that was difficult to use and therefore impaired the users' work safety [6].

In the case of emergency response work, studies show that the design of information technology for crisis and emergency response must address the field operative

J. Löffler and M. Klann (Eds.): Mobile Response, LNCS 5424, pp. 122–129, 2009.

challenges of using information technology [4]. Neglecting to do so will not only have consequences on the field operative level but also reducing the overall value of such technology. The major challenge is not to make the technology work, but to work with the technology. The study shows that there is a tension between information technology use and time-criticality in emergency response work.

3 Research Approach

This paper reports from two projects where two Swedish fire and rescue services have tested and evaluated commercial mobile incident support systems. The research approach adopted in this study was qualitative with ethnography [3] as the primary vehicle to gain detailed insights and rich descriptions of information technology use in these specific work settings.

3.1 Data Collection and Analytical Perspective

The data collection techniques includes from observations, interviews and video recordings from field experiments. In each organization, one fire crew has been interviewed before the system evaluation started to identify the expectations they had on the system. Several interviews have been made during the evaluation period and a final interview with each user group has been made in the end of the evaluation period.

The data collected during the study was analyzed from a user-centered design perspective and influenced by a collaborative work perspective. This meant that the analysis is heavily focused on the end-users perspectives and experiences of the system. Accordingly, very little efforts have been spent on trying to understand the underlying assumptions and design decisions made by the system vendors.

The argument of having a strong focus on the users is based on the understanding that this particular user group (i.e firefighters) tend to have an informal use-mandate [4] giving them a strong veto about deciding what technology is suitable for use in field operative work and which is not. How the users experience specific technology is therefore of outmost importance in order to be successful in a future large-scale deployment of technology in these organizations.

3.2 Brief Description of the Two Organizations/Projects

Organization/project A. This project was run by one of the largest fire and rescue services having 11 full-time fire stations and around 80 firefighters on 24-hours standby. This organization made a decision in 2006 to start to investigate how mobile information technology could provide support in the field operative work. The organization had at this moment participated for several years in a research project focusing on mobile IT for field operative work. Now was the moment to start a test and evaluation project of a commercial mobile incident support system.

The commercial system (here named Penta), was provided by a minor system vendor based in Sweden. The author of this paper was at the time conducting research together with the rescue services organization regarding mobile IT-use for field operative work. As a consequence, the author also got access to participate in this test and evaluation phases of the project.

Organization/project B. This project was run by medium-size fire and rescue services having 2 full-time fire stations and around 12 firefighters on 24-hours standby. In 2006, the organization made a decision to test and evaluate a commercial mobile incident support system. The commercial system (here named Octa), was provided by a large European security systems vendor. The author of this paper was at the time contacted by the system vendor and a research contract was established allowing the author to participate in the project to study the test and evaluation phases.

3.3 Description of the Mobile Incident Support Systems

Mobile incident support systems have during the last few years received increasing attention by fire and rescue services in Sweden. A range of system vendors has developed various solutions that target the needs in operative emergency response work. Mobile incident support system consists of a set of applications integrated into one system with the objective to support a range of task in the operative response work. Mobile incident command systems include applications for navigational support, access to maps, predefined response plans, property information and access to hazardous material databases. Response-plans consist of textual descriptions of the property, information about the business activities, name and phone number to contact persons, specific risks or hazard material, pre-determined entry-points to the buildings and availability of fire hydrants on the accident location. It also includes photos and/or schematic drawings of the buildings on the property.

The two projects in focus in this paper, involves systems with similar functionality. Only minor functionality in the systems differs between the two systems. The focus in this paper is not the specific functionality but the lessons learned.

4   Results

The result from the two projects covers many areas and topics, but the fundamental and common issues could be summarized as the following two categories:

- Range of functionality versus depth of content
- Inconsistent interaction models

4.1 Range of Functionality Versus Depth of Content

This category highlights the problem between balancing the range of functionality to be included in a system and the depth of content provide by a system. In both projects the users (fire crew and fire crew commander) identified that the system did more than well cover the functionality needed. Both systems included functionality that typically addresses tasks embedded in the work phases [4] of mobilization and intervention. For mobilization including enroute activities, the systems provided information about the alarm, street address and route advice. The user could here zoom in on locations, switch between current location and target location, switch between map data and aerial photos, search for property information and peripheral property information. But, they also mentioned that a majority of the functionality would seldom come to use due to the limited time available for interacting with the system.

For the intervention phase the system provided functionality to view building blueprints, detailed property information as well as phone numbers to property representatives, and access to detailed hazard material information. Having said this, the systems clearly consisted of functionality that one typically would expect emergency responders to request. The systems did well enough cover the general information needs for emergency response.

However, having general information needs fulfilled did not equal to being fully satisfied with the system. The system did provide functionality to make available information understood as critical, but the users were very critical against the depth of content provided by the system.

Coverage of Property Data

From their perspective, the system did not meet their requirements concerning information coverage. A clear example of this was the lack of coverage of property information. Only a small number of properties in their district had detailed property information assigned.

> IC: We have a system with a map and alot of nice functionality, but no information on the properties. I mean, when I get an alarm such as a fire in a school, then I would like to see information for that specific school. Just based on the address. I would like to verify if there are any risk and stuff like that. During this test period, we have had no time to transfer such information into the system. Basically, the system becomes an expensive navigator.

The above excerpt indicate that during the test period, the organization failed to provide the necessary information regarding properties which therefore reduced the system to only function as a navigator. The lack of information in the system negatively influenced the experience of the entire system. The lack of information was not a system related problem but became a system related problem due to the experience of the users that the system was empty and did not provide critical support.

In cases when the system did provide property information, additional problems were experienced. The property information was not designed for mobile use in time-critical work. Property information was imported from a system used by fire inspectors that make inspections of properties in order to verify the fire safety. The consequence of this was that the property information was too detailed and covered aspects of minor interest for a fire crew and fire crew commander. In the vast amount of information, sections of important information became hidden. This meant that even if the information was available, it was not accessible in the specific context. The lack of appropriate designed information resulted in having the users experiencing that the system did not provide this type of information in a format to be quickly consumed.

The use of aerial maps have in the recent years become very popular in fire and rescue services for risk assessment and even just as a tool for learning more about the local district. The use of aerial maps in a mobile incident support system was therefore a requirement. Firefighters and fire crew commanders would in such system use the aerial maps to get a more detailed birds-eye view over specific locations. The key benefit of such data would help them to see building sections, alternative routes as well as more insights on how a specific facility was outlined. However, having access to aerial maps is not the same as having access to aerial maps of enough resolution. The aerial maps available in the tests covered in this paper did not have the quality to comply with the level of details required by the users. The following excerpts show a conversation during a field test when the level of detail was insufficient.

Instructor:	go to the incident
Fire crew commander:	okay, here is the location, building on fire
Instructor:	click on orthophoto [aerial map]
Fire crew commander:	Okay
Instructor:	Now you can determine the type of building you have there on this alarm
Instructor:	I believe you can zoom in a bit more
Fire crew commander:	zoom in… here…
Instructor:	hmm, no…it was not possible to go into more detail, I´m sorry

The results from the two projects show that in the preparations prior the start of the two projects, too much had been focused on the range of functionality but to a large extent ignored the depth of content.

4.2   Inconsistent Interaction Model

This category highlights the problem of inconsistent interaction models, which affects the user experience in a time-critical work setting. The analysis of user's interacting with the systems show that the systems lack a consistent interaction model.

The primary application for the systems was a map interface with a range of buttons on toolbars on the left hand side and on top of the screen layout. Each button was labeled with distinct names signaling the underlying functionality. Even if the users to some extent had problems to click on these buttons while using the application in the vehicle while driving to a location, they did manage to point their index finger a click on a button. However, what did confuse the users and presented critical challenges to the users was that some interaction features was embedded in the map. Some

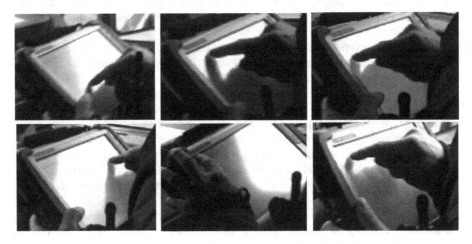

Fig. 1. Interaction across the entire application window

functionality was available not only via the buttons, but also by clicking on the map. The functionality was linked to specific types of symbols as well as specific finger movements on the map. In contrast to buttons, embedded features in a map is not as visible and distinct as buttons. The combinations of interaction models also resulted in a situation where the user had access to specific functionality that was spread across the entire application window. The following photos from a field test illustrate the situation of indistinct interaction features.

Our studies has shown that there seems to be a steep learning curve in order to fully understand when interaction should take place via existing buttons or whether the functionality will be available via the map. Even if this could be seen as a trivial problem, one should keep in mind that this specific user group only has very limited time-cycles for interaction with information technology.

Further, when clicking on an item in a list-box to view property information, a new application was launched to present the information in a PDF-document. The time-delay to launch the new application as well as having the new application on-top of the map was a negative experience by the users. When a PDF-document was opened in the mobile incident support system, a traditional PDF-reader was launched and positioned on top of the existing mobile incident support application, causing some confusion. Users experienced that they had not launched this external application and could in some cases spend considerable time just make sense of the new application that to a large extent blocked the access to the underlying map functionality. This illustrates a weakness in the integration of the external application and the mobile incident system and the external application.

The end-users did also experience significant problems to interact, using a finger on the touch screen, with the application providing the PDF-document property information. This application was an off-the-shelf product typically designed for keyboard and mouse interaction, and not for touch-screen interaction in a mobile work context.

5 Discussion

The results outlined in this paper address two major challenges in designing information technology for the time-critical work of emergency response. The problems presented are well known within the HCI-community but according to the results presented here, difficult to address by system vendors. The problem is probably not that the system vendors lack knowledge in interaction design, but rather, they lack detailed knowledge about the work practice. This means, from a technical perspective they have good competence in designing and developing systems that works or is functional on a technical level. But from a user perspective the system is difficult to work with. One could argue that the users can learn to use the system specific interaction but considering the very short time these systems actually are in use in emergency response work, the problems with inconsistent interaction models becomes critical.

Many of the issues reported of in this paper could have been avoided by using some form of participatory design approach. Such approach would have provided early feedback to the system vendors regarding critical aspects that make a difference in time-critical interaction. So why did the system vendors not involve end-users? A clue to the answer could be found in very idea of these development efforts. The focus was on new technical features and innovative functionality. These factors make a piece of software sellable. The lack of involvement of users is related to the strong focus on developing functionality and reaching a deadline within a specific budget. The interaction design and specifically interaction design that takes into account work practice specific issues has less priority. System vendors sell innovative software not innovative use of software. The two systems covered in this paper did not have an obviously poor interaction design. But the lack of knowledge of how small detailed aspects influences the use of the system, became evident first when putting the systems into the hand of real users, in real organizations, and in realistic use settings.

A similar problem is also found in our very own research community, we as a community tend to focus on innovative functionality that improves interaction. We focus less often on the information that our applications provide or the use of such information in a given work context. There is a clear lack of performance metrics for how well a given design conforms to a specific work practice.

It could be argued that the system vendors as well as the research community, too often design information technology that becomes de-contextualized. There are only a few examples of projects and studies that pay attention to the fine-grained details in emergency response work practices and carefully embed them in their system design [1, 2].

The results presented in this paper illustrate this general problem. The advice for the future is that both industrial system developers as well as design-oriented researchers should adopt and further extend participatory design methods in order to avoid de-contextualised solutions that will conflict to or obstruct in a given work practice.

6   Conclusions

This paper has outlined results from two projects where local fire and rescue services have evaluated commercial mobile incident support systems. The results from the study of these projects show the need to better accommodate for a user-centered design in order to avoid information technology that is challenging to use in time-critical work.

The results illustrate two key problems; balancing the range of functionality versus content depth, and inconsistent interaction model. Industrial developers as well as design-oriented researchers face the same risk of overemphasis innovative features instead of paying attention to aspects in the work practice that may or may not conflict with the proposed design.

One approach to avoid or limit such problems and the need of costly redesign late in the design work could be by adopting participatory design.

Acknowledgements

I would like to thank the two Fire & Rescue Services involved in this study, as well as the two system vendors and the Swedish Rescue Services Agency.

References

1. Büscher, M.: Interaction in motion: Embodied conduct in emergency teamwork. In: Online Multimedia Proceedings of the 2nd International Society for Gesture Studies Conference 'Interacting Bodies'. Lyon, France (2005)
2. Denef, S., Ramirez, L., Dyrks, T., Stevens, G.: Handy Navigation in Ever-Changing Spaces — an Ethnographic Study of Firefighting Practices Designing Interactive Systems, Cap Town, South Africa (2008)
3. Hammersley, M., Atkinson, P.: Ethnography, 2nd edn. Routledge, London (1995)
4. Landgren, J.: Designing information technology for emergency response. PhD-thesis. Gothenburg Studies in Informatics, report 39. Gothenburg University (2007)
5. Landgren, J.: Investigating the tension between information technology use and emergency response Work. In: The proceedings of the European Conference on Information Systems (ECIS 2007), St Gallen, Switzerland (2007)
6. Marcus, A., Gasperini, J.: Almost dead on arrival: a case study of non-user-centered design for a police emergency-response system. Interactions 13(5) (2006)
7. Quarantelli, E.L.: Problematical aspects of the information/communication revolution for disaster planning and research: ten non-technical issues and questions. Disaster Prevention and Management 6(2), 94–106 (1997)

TwiddleNet: Smartphones as Personal Content Servers for First Responders

Gurminder Singh and Dirk Ableiter

Naval Postgraduate School, Department of Computer Science
Monterey, California 93943, USA
gsingh@nps.edu

Abstract. TwiddleNet uses smartphones as personal servers to enable instant content capture and dissemination for first-responders. It supports the information sharing needs of first responders in the early stages of an emergency response operation. In TwiddleNet, content, once captured, is automatically tagged and disseminated using one of the several networking channels available in smartphones. TwiddleNet pays special attention to minimizing the equipment, network set-up time, and content capture and dissemination effort. It can support small teams of emergency responders in the first 48-72 hours of an emergency response by using smartphone-based infrastructure and scale up to handle a much larger number of users with a more robust backend.

Keywords: Emergency Services, Military Information Systems, Distributed Information Systems.

1 Introduction

The modern smartphones are beginning to match the computing, storage and networking capability of desktop PCs of just a few years ago. This has led researchers to start viewing these devices as their personal servers [2, 9] or their primary computing devices [1]. Since smartphones are small and light-weight, they are good vehicles for making computing mobile.

Additionally, smartphones have already exceeded the content capture capability of PCs! Most smartphones come pre-equipped with cameras and microphones enabling users to capture pictures, videos and sounds. PCs have usually not been equipped with this capability, and given their size and weight, cannot be used in mobile settings anyway. The combination of computing, networking, storage and content capture capability of smartphones can lead to new ways of sharing content. This combined capability of smartphones has been ignored by all of the previous efforts which have focused exclusively on computing, networking and storage.

We have developed a system called TwiddleNet which harnesses the power of smartphones to enable 1) instant content capture and dissemination, 2) owner control of content, and 3) search, view and downloading of content. The system comprises a smartphone acting as a portal, which enables connectivity among other smartphones acting as clients. Client devices can work either as personal content servers or as

J. Löffler and M. Klann (Eds.): Mobile Response, LNCS 5424, pp. 130–137, 2009.
© Springer-Verlag Berlin Heidelberg 2009

content requesters, and they can switch between these roles rather transparently to the user. When acting as a server, a TwiddleNet smartphone tags content upon capture, packages it as an Atom feed and sends it to the portal. This entire process is fully automated and works in real time. When acting as a content requester, a TwiddleNet smartphone receives Atom feeds [6] generated by the personal servers of other users. Content can be received in two modes. First, the user can pull the desired content by browsing or searching through the various feeds available. The second option is to register user interests with the portal and have the content be pushed by the appropriate server automatically. Note that the portal is merely a gateway for TwiddleNet smartphones. By default, the portal does not store nor serve content. In special circumstances, clients may ask the portal to be proxy for them.

TwiddleNet capabilities are tuned to the content sharing needs of first responders. It is designed to support the first 48-72 hours of first responder missions. As a result, TwiddleNet assumes little infrastructure and provides sufficient redundancy to operate on alternate mechanisms. After the initial response period, it is assumed that there would be better infrastructure and more support available. The system can be scaled up or down depending on the needs of the mission. The entire system can be run on smartphones to support a small first-responder team, or on a mix of smartphones and server-class computers to link together a large number of users sharing pictures, videos, audio and mobile-blogs.

Key first responder requirements that TwiddleNet addresses are as follows:

- **Quick Set-Up.** A key requirement of first responders, especially immediately after a disaster has struck, is to get going with their mission at the fastest speed possible. This means little time to set-up. The entire TwiddleNet system is designed to work with light-weight and battery-powered equipment. TwiddleNet fly-away kits, as explained later, include everything that the first responder team will need to get started with their mission.

- **Tight-loop, Frequent Communication.** An important task of first responders is to convey the ground reality to their co-workers and the control room. This needs to be done frequently and in real-time but without taking too much of the first responders' time and attention lest it start affecting their mission performance. To support this requirement, TwiddleNet-enabled smartphones produce tagged, xml-based, Atom feeds automatically on content capture. The entire process of generating and attaching tags to content is automated. Once content has been captured and tagged, the content is pushed automatically to those who need it and notices are disseminated to others so they can pull the content if desired.

- **Light-Weight Equipment.** Mobility is often an integral part of the first responders work. As a result, their equipment must be as light as possible. TwiddleNet uses smartphones, which are light-weight and small, but still provide the redundancy that is so critical to the mission success. In addition, the TwiddleNet portal itself can be run on handheld devices (PDAs or small handheld computers) to further reduce the weight that the first responder team needs to carry.

- **Scale-up as Team/Requirements Grow.** TwiddleNet is focused on the first 48-72 hours after a disaster, when the team size is small. As the situation evolves and the team size grows, TwiddleNet can hand-off to a more robust infrastructure (powerful servers) when it becomes available.

- **Power.** Due to their short charge life and weight, batteries that power the smartphones are an important conern. Often first responders have to carry spare batteries, which increase the weight they have to carry. To address this issue, TwiddleNet pays special attention to power management - it supports smart caching of popular content provided owner consents. It allows the first responder to offload some of its serving functions to the TwiddleNet portal. In addition, to further conserve power, TwiddleNet supports several user-selectable content dissemination schemes.

The focus of this paper is to describe the overall architecture of TwiddleNet and present its key capabilities.

2 Related Work

The dramatic increase in the compute power and miniaturization of electronic components has lead to small, light-weight, battery-powered devices which can perform a significant amount of computing for the user. Want et al [9] envisioned such devices without traditional I/O capabilities to act as user's mobile personal server. When needed, the user could use the I/O capabilities of external devices such as desk/laptop computers to get access to information in the personal server through a Bluetooth connection. Intel's personal media server project [4] extends Want et al's [9] original personal server concept by making it phone-based and using it as a personal media server.

BluOnyx (www.bluonyx.com) is a commercial realization of Want et al's [9] vision of a personal server. It is a cell phone-sized mobile content server product from Agere Systems [5]. The system provides network connectivity with Bluetooth and WiFi, and enables users to store pictures, videos, music, emails and other files. BluOnyx does not have a screen but the resident content can be viewed/played on the cell phone, TV or PC screens. In its capability and form factor, it is what Want et al [9] had envisioned a personal server to be.

Byland and Segall [2] investigate the use of personal servers running on smartphones to support seamless mobility. They investigate requirements from not only computing but network and user interface perspectives as well. In their analysis, in addition to mobile servers, they explore the use of remote personal servers to provide support for seamless mobility.

Barton, Zhai and Cousins [1] propose the use of cell phones equipped with large storage, in the range of a terabyte, to support mobile users in a variety of work as well entertainment tasks. Following [9] and [2], they envision these devices to use and take advantage of the large displays of PCs and televisions.

The common thread among all of the above efforts is that they all recognize that the user can carry significant compute and storage capability; that multiple networking modalities, many more than available in PCs, have become available in the small devices; and, that when possible mobile devices should use comfortable displays and keyboards of PCs. None of these efforts exploite the content capture capability of smartphones the way TwiddleNet does. Instead of viewing smartphone as compute devices with limited screens and no keyboards, TwiddleNet views them as tools for content capture and dissemination. Another difference between TwiddleNet and previous efforts is that TwiddleNet creates a complete network among personal server devices rather than as stand-alone, personal servers only.

IBM's Infinity [3] is a middleware framework for linking heterogeneous mobile devices. By doing so, it enables access to content resident on mobile devices. At a high-level the goals of TwiddleNet are similar to that of Infinity – both focus on enabling access to content on mobile devices. The most significant difference between the two systems is that TwiddleNet treats smartphones as personal servers and provides a portal front-end to enable content access whereas Infinity is middleware to develop general data sharing applications for smartphones. Infinity will be good toolkit to develop TwiddleNet.

Q121 (www.q121.com), a social networking and media-sharing service, allows people who register with the service to upload their favorite songs, videos, and photos to the site and then send them to the cell phones of other registered users [9]. In many respects Q121 is similar to other popular services such as MySpace (www.myspace.com) and FaceBook (www.facebook.com) which also allow people to upload their content and share with others with one significant difference – Q121 focuses on cell phones rather than everyday computers. While Q121 and TwiddleNet both focus on cell phones, TwiddleNet treats cell phones as personal content servers rather than content capture and upload devices for the web.

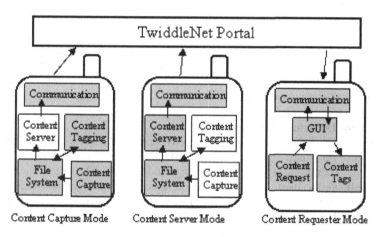

Fig. 1. TwiddleNet Clients

3   TwiddleNet Architecture

In TwiddleNet, all client devices can work either as personal content servers or as content requesters, and they can switch between these roles rather transparently to the user (Figure 1). In the content server mode, the client device captures new content, tags it and lets the TwiddleNet portal know that the content is available by sending an Atom feed out. The feed tells the portal, and through it to the rest of user population, what is available on a particular content server. In the content requester mode, the client device gets updates from the TwiddleNet portal and request select content from the other users' client devices operating in the content server mode.

The TwiddleNet portal is a central repository for meta-data (or feeds) generated by clients. It allows for centralized searching for desired content as well as for sending alerts when a match occurs. The portal is designed to also act as a cache for frequently accessed content. In the following sections, we provide an overview of the significant modules of the TwiddleNet architecture.

3.1 Client

A typical TwiddleNet client is a smartphone but it is possible to use PDAs equipped with required networking and content capture capabilities as well.

3.1.1 Content Tagging in Client

The TwiddleNet client relies on an XML provisioning document to build its metadata files. This provisioning document contains all of the tags that could possibly appear when providing metadata about shared content. Each base tag has attributes that the application reads as a set of instructions detailing how the tag is to be handled, i.e., how a tag value is to be generated, when a tag value is to be generated and if a tag is mandated to appear in the finished metadata document. There are additional tags that facilitate processing, but the key tag attributes are how (either automatic or userdefined), when (corresponding to the lifetime stages of the entry: predefined, onGeneration, and onSending) and authority (either mandatory or optional). The combination of these attributes yields 12 possible tag types; however, for purposes of TwiddleNet two of those types are never provisioned (userdefined/mandatory/onGeneration and userdefined/mandatory /onSend). The TwiddleNet client builds metadata entries according to the Atom syndication standard. As metadata files are transmitted, they are added to an Atom feed maintained by the device.

3.1.2 Content Dissemination from Client

TwiddleNet provides the user with five different options for when they can send their updates. These options include sending on a timed interval, content generation, delayed content generation, sensing a connection and manual. The timed interval sending option allows the user to send updates at user set timer intervals such as every hour or every ten hours. The feature is adjustable from 1 minute to 999 hours. This feature allows the user to collect content during the time interval without having to worry about sending them. It also allows for the collection of many pieces of content to be sent at one time vice being sent one at a time. The on-generation sending feature allows for automatic sending of files as soon as they are either created or added to the shared folder. This feature allows the user to automatically update the portal with information as soon as it is created. Although this is not ideal for power conservation it is ideal in situations where timeliness is an issue. Sending content on delayed generation is an attempt to gain the power saving benefits of sending many pieces of content at once while still maintaining the real-time benefits of the application. The feature activates a timer when content is generated. During this period if another piece of content is generated the timer is reset to its original value, this continues until the timer expires at which time the new contents are all sent together. This feature is ideal when the user takes pictures in clusters. Say for instance a user saw a site of interest and is going to take many pictures a minute or two apart, the delayed sending feature would allow far all of the pictures to be collected and their documents to be sent after the picture taking was complete. The sending whenever a new connection is sensed by the device (useful when you have spotty coverage), and manually sending.

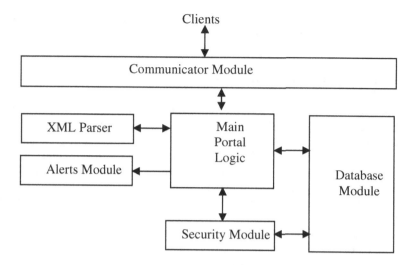

Fig. 2. TwiddleNet Portal Architecture

3.2 TwiddleNet Portal

Figure 2 shows the key components of the TwiddleNet portal. For a small first responder team, the TwiddleNet portal is able to run on a smartphone Windows Mobile 5.0. With this implementation, there is little set-up required as everything runs on handheld devices. When the size of the team grows, the portal can be moved to the standard server hardware. Apache 2.2.4 has been used on the standard server implementation of the portal, while the smartphone implementation is based on the vxWeb server by Cambridge Computer Corporation.

Portal allows for users to subscribe to desired content and receive alerts when new content, which was previously subscribed to, is created and made available. The web interface to the portal allows users to perform searches on all available content from all registered TwiddleNet clients. The Portal supplies hyperlinks of desired content to TwiddleNet clients. A more robust Portal should allow for users to cache frequently requested data on the portal to ease demand placed on the small devices.

4   TwiddleNet Fly-Away Kits

A key feature of TwiddleNet is its ability to work with several different communication modalities as long as IP is supported. This enables us to provide a fail-safe system when needed, and if all network modalities are operational, some of the channels can be used for non-TwiddleNet communication, such as making voice calls, sending SMS etc. In order to deal with the eventuality that there is no Wireless WAN available, we have made a complete fly-away kit. This kit includes everything that a team needs in case absolutely no infrastructure exists at the scene of emergency. The kit includes several smartphones configured with the TwiddleNet capability, a battery-powered BGAN (Broadband Global Area Network) unit, and a smartphone working as the TwiddleNet portal.

5 Current Status and Future Work

The current implementation of TwiddleNet runs on Windows Mobile5.0 smartphones. It has been tested with TwiddleNet portal running on an iPAQ as well as on a standard PC server. In addition to the modules described above, a mobile command center has also been developed. It enables the operators in the command center to receive and view content captured by all members of the team, and thus have a complete view of the situation faced by the first responders.

We are currently focused on developing modules for privacy and security of the system.

We have done the first field test of TwiddleNet in Operation Golden Phoenix [7] which simulated a 7.9 earthquake scenario in Los Angles, California and had the participation of several agencies including LAPD, LAFD, LA Co. Sheriff, LA Co. Fire, California National Guard, MAG-46, NPS and SPAWAR. TwiddleNet was tested by soldiers from the US Marine Corps. Their overall feedback was very encouraging. In addition to ruggedizing the device, some of their other suggestions for improvements included a better user interface and more focus on privacy and security.

We have also developed a first version of a Mobile Command Post (MCP) for TwiddleNet. MCP is implemented as an authoritative source of all TwiddleNet content. This can be used for a several purposes: to keep the mission command appraised of the ground reality in real-time, to push important content out to the entire or select parts of the team, and to act as an achieve of content for post mission analysis and report.

6 Conclusions

In TwiddleNet, we have presented a way of harnessing the entire power of smartphones, including their content capture capability. TwiddleNet treats smartphones as live content feeds to enable immediate content capture and dissemination.

Emergency operations require the first responders to accomplish difficult tasks under high stress conditions. Technology should allow them to focus on their task without burdening them with peculiarities of the communication devices. The first responders need to communicate effectively, efficiently and frequently. This is often critical to success of their mission. TwiddleNet supports such communication requirements without getting in the way of their work.

Acknowledgements

This work has benefited from the participation of several students at NPS including MAJ Jon Towle, CAPT Rob Myers, CAPT Eddie Zapata, LT Chris Clotfelter, and LT Antonios Rimikis.

References

1. Barton, J.J., Zhai, S., Cousins, S.B.: Mobile Phones Will Become The Primary Personal Computing Device. In: Proc. 7th IEEE Workshop on Mobile Computing Systems & Applications (2006)
2. Bylund, M., Segall, Z.: Towards seamless mobility with personal servers. Info – The Journal of policy, regulation and strategy for telecommunications 6(3), 172–179 (2004)
3. Cheung, A., Grandison, T., Johnson, H., Schönauer, S.: Ínfïnïty: A Generic Platform for Application Development and Information Sharing on Mobile Devices. In: Sixth International ACM Workshop on Data Engineering for Wireless and Mobile Access (MobiDE) 2007, Beijing, China (June 2007)
4. Intel Personal Media Server (2004) (accessed October 22, 2007),
   `http://www.intel.com/research/exploratory/personal_server.htm`
5. McGrath, D.: Agere 'card' server streams content to devices. EE Times (December 18, 2006) (accessed on October 22, 2007),
   `http://www.eetimes.com/news/semi/showArticle.jhtml;jsessionid =4DSCXNJPLTOYYQSNDLPSKH0CJUNN2JVN?articleID=196700349`
6. Nottingham, M., Sayre, R. (eds.) The Atom Syndication Format. IETF RFC4287 (December 2005)
7. OGP, Operation Golden Phoenix in California (July 16-26, 2007) (accessed on October 23, 2007), `http://ncorp.org/old/showarticle.php?articleID=5847`
8. Roush, W.: A New Platform for Social Computing: Cell Phones. Technology Review (July 3, 2006),
   `http://www.techreview.com/ read_article.aspx?ch=specialsections&sc=telecom&id=17079`
9. Want, R., Pering, T., Danneels, G., Kumar, M., Sundar, M., Light, J.: The Personal Server: Changing the Way We Think about Ubiquitous Computing. In: Borriello, G., Holmquist, L.E. (eds.) UbiComp 2002. LNCS, vol. 2498, pp. 194–209. Springer, Heidelberg (2002)

Secure and Reliable Communication Infrastructure for a Distributed IT-Federation

Thang Tran, Kai Daniel, and Christian Wietfeld

Communication Networks Institute
Dortmund University of Technology
44227 Dortmund, Germany
{Thang.Tran,Kai.Daniel,Christian.Wietfeld}@tu-dortmund.de

Abstract. One of today's major problems is the lack of detailed and current information on the spot for fire brigades and other action forces (e.g. police). However, access to the distributed information (e.g. location maps of fire hydrants, building plans, air photos) is not always available and has to be requested via paper mail in advance. Particularly, preventive fire protection and reactive fire prevention depending on a high-quality information management, which allows them to arrange a more efficient operation. In order to solve this problem, this paper proposes a design of a secure and reliable role based concept, which permits fast access to confidential information. Furthermore, the technical challenge of the development of such a communication infrastructure is illustrated. A performance analysis of an exemplary Monitoring Service for a distributed IT-Federation is introduced, in which an analytical Boolean Reliability Model is presented as an approach to visualize the bottleneck of a decentralized system.

Keywords: IT-Federation, Authentication, Authorization, Role Based Access Control (RBAC), Single Sign-On (SSO).

1 Introduction

1.1 Use Case and Problem

For huge organizations the simultaneous access to information held in distributed databases is still a challenge, if requirements like high performance, security, reliability and simplicity have to be fulfilled concurrently [1]. These requirements have been addressed in the German research project "Mobile Information System for Process Optimization in Fire Brigades and Public Authorities (MobisPro)" funded by the German Federal Ministry of Economics and Technology in cooperation with one of the largest fire brigades in Germany / Dortmund with 1,300 fire fighters and 30,000 operations per annum.

In large rescue operations all participating rescue forces need detailed information about the situation at the scene, for example

- object, building and site plans
- address lists from registration offices

J. Löffler and M. Klann (Eds.): Mobile Response, LNCS 5424, pp. 138–147, 2009.

- table of hydrants
- plans of (gas) pipelines
- table of dangerous substances
- video sequences (made by drones or fire fighters) or
- manufacturer information about car body works (car accidents)

Today fire brigades own summarized information sheets of the most important buildings and objects in their field of responsibility that are always held on the fire-fighting vehicle.

However, this results in insufficient information for the rescue workers during rescue operations. The time needed for receiving essential and not outdated information in the field of danger and fire defense can decide on life or death. Figure 1 shows the long process of information retrieval in current reactive fire prevention.

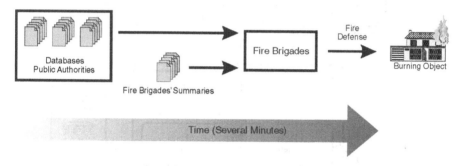

Fig. 1. Process of information retrieval in current reactive fire prevention

The process at the preventive fire protection has to be also optimized [1]. Particularly, the paper mails require several days in some cases (see fig. 2). Therefore, the general goal is to accelerate the process of information provision by information hosts respectively different public authorities / information systems. Additionally, the distribution of information at the incident scene itself can be solved with the group communication concept as presented in [2].

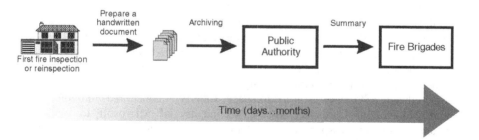

Fig. 2. Process of information retrieval in current preventive fire protection

2 Technical Challenge and Approach

A communication platform is needed in order to enable the interoperability of heterogenous and distributed information systems. Figure 3 shows the approach for a secure and reliable communication infrastructure.

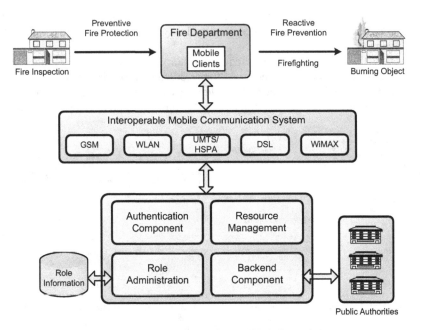

Fig. 3. Communication platform for mobile information systems

Detailed information about the incident scene is required, which are unfortunately located on different and distributed information systems. To receive essential information the user needs to authenticate for each system individually and repeatedly (see fig. 4a). As disadvantage, each user has to remember the access data for each system. For this reason, Single Sign-On (SSO) systems bring helpful authentication mechanisms.

On the one hand, the main advantage of a SSO system is the ease of use since only one account is needed to ensure the access to distributed information systems (cf. fig. 4b). On the other hand, e.g. in the case of man-in-the-middle attack which allows an attacker to gain full access to all data of the information system. In Figure 3 the Backend Component represents the SSO functionality.

Some current SSO systems are Cardspace, Liberty Alliance and Shibboleth. The Identity Metasystem Cardspace is the second try of Microsoft to avoid the disadvantages of .Net Passport, which is based on Web Service technologies and can be used without special licensing. An Open Source at Microsoft is also available, but it is not platform independent at present [3].

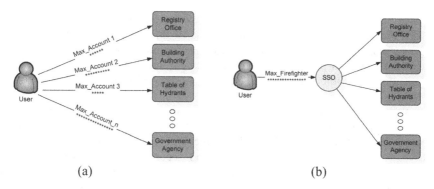

Fig. 4. Access without SSO (a) and with SSO (b)

Liberty Alliance Project is a consortium composed of well-known companies, which was founded by Sun Microsystem as competition to .Net Passport. They target the definition of processes for federated identities, single sign-on and related protocols (e.g. XMLSec, Openssl), which had a strong influence on the specification of the IT-security SAML (Security Assertion Markup Language Protocol) [4].

Shibboleth is an SSO system for distributed authentication and authorization and presents the implementation of SAML specification, more precisely the Web Browser SSO profile. The developer of Shibboleth is the Internet2 consortium, which consists of about 200 US universities and industrial partners. Shibboleth applies technologies like XML, HTTP, SOAP [5].

For a fast and efficient information search an appropriate service is offered, which generates a clear visualization of the conglomerated and distributed information. In addition to the fast search service a role based access model is required to reduce the administrative overhead [6]. It is used for the user and role administration (see fig. 3). Figure 5 depicts an example for the relation between roles and rights. The role component is shown as the role administration in Figure 3.

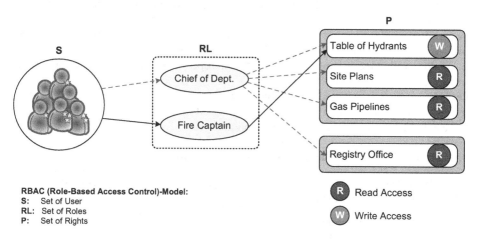

Fig. 5. Access Control using RBAC model

Security requirements are necessary due to the handling of confidential data (e.g. registry office). In order to control the process of information provision during an emergency response, authentication and authorization methods have to be considered in the communication platform. One of the current suited IT-security protocols for authentication and authorization is the Security Assertion Markup Language Protocol (SAML).

The standardized and XML-based IT-security SAML protocol is deployed by the OASIS consortium, which specifies the secure information transmission between the communication partners. The SAML framework enables the single sign on functionality to assure the interoperability and secure communication within and across organizational boundaries on the internet, in which the SOAP protocol is used for carrying SAML messages [7]. Moreover, SAML uses a public key infrastructure (PKI) to guarantee the authenticity (certificates), confidentiality (encryption) and data integrity. The PKI applies the Transport Layer Security (TLS) to encode the data transmission and assure the data integrity and authenticity [8].

The high availability of the communication platform plays an important role in the reactive fire prevention to ensure the seamless provision of relevant information from different information systems. Consequently, a routing protocol / resource management (see fig. 3) is required, which automatically choose the best communication way (e.g. UMTS, WLAN, WiMAX). The routing protocol will run on a mobile device (e.g. handheld, PDA, laptop) with multiple wireless interfaces. Reference to some existing vertical handover technologies are Mobile IP [9] and SCTP [10], which have to be adapted for this communication platform.

In the case of a write process, especially in a preventing fire protection, a prioritization concept is needed in order to avoid data inconsistency, if several authorized users want to modify the same data concurrently.

3 Example: Distributed Monitoring Service

The today's topics data privacy and security are more and more important. For a high acceptance and due to lawful proofs a Monitoring Service for distributed information systems are consequently required to make the traceability of user activities faster and easier. Especially, this service is very helpful to obtain a fast and summarized overview about a certain user activity from a distributed IT-Federation.

In the following chapter the novel interoperability concept and prototype implementation for a Role Based SSO (RB-SSO) communication platform is described which is adapted from Shibboleth because of its secure, free and open implementation. The employed Shibboleth is based on SAML 1.1. Since March 2008 there exists a current stable release of Shibboleth with SAML 2.0 [5].

3.1 System Architecture and Role Based Monitoring Service

The SW architecture of the communication platform (see fig. 6) consists of the following three system modules

- Identity Provider (IDP)
- Service Provider (SP)
- Clients

Generally, the Identity Provider (see fig. 6) manages the user authentication for the whole IT-Federation and the SPs are represented by the public authorities or information systems, e.g. registry office, building authorities or government agencies. In order to control the authorization process each SP has a Shibboleth Service Protection (cf. fig. 6). User clients are SmartPhones or Laptops for instance.

3.1.1 Role Based Monitoring Service

The Role Based SSO (RB-SSO) communication platform has to be enhanced by the distributed Monitoring Service due to lawful proofs. Thus the system comprises of the following three modules

- Local Monitoring Service (LMS)
- Global Monitoring Service (GMS)
- Interface for global Monitoring Service (IGMS)

that will be described in more detail in the next paragraphs.

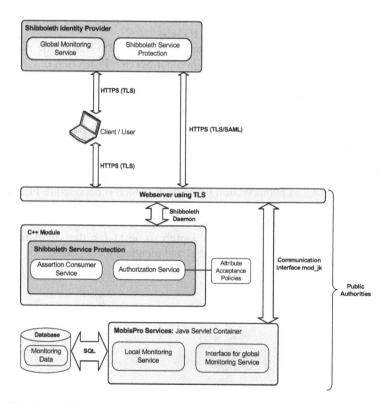

Fig. 6. RB-SSO communication platform enhanced by the Monitoring Service

Local Monitoring Service (LMS)

The Local Monitoring Service located on the SP (see fig. 6) traces the authentication, authorization procedures and user activities on the information systems. To proof all unambiguous operations each user action within the information system is recorded locally by every LMS with date, time and kind of process, which are finally saved in the database (e.g. MySQL). Kind of processes are e.g. read, write, date of authentication, username and modification date of appropriate data.

Global Monitoring Service (GMS)

The recorded data is located on distributed databases, which make it very inconvenient and annoying to search and monitor repeatedly and manually for keep track of user changes. For that reason, the Global Monitoring Service (see fig. 6) supports a fast and efficient search in all connected information systems within the IT-Federation. GMS provides a search mask to the user that allows to search for parameters like username, date and time. The search results are then shown to the user in a summarized way.

Considering the security, the GMS can only be used if an authorized user has been authenticated by the IDP before.

Interface for global Monitoring Service (IGMS)

The IGMS of SP receives the search parameters from GMS. Before the appropriate user can get response from IGMS, the Shibboleth Service Protection of SP requests the IDP using the SAML-Protocol, if the user is already authenticated and has access rights. After receiving the response from IDP and if the user has the rights, the search results are subsequently transmitted to the GMS via HTTPS.

4   Performance Analysis

A testbed has been set up for the performance measurement of the average response time of authentication and authorization procedures, which is depicted in Figure 7.

The communication technology UMTS has been chosen. On the right side of the figure the IDP, authority and registration office shape the RB-SSO communication platform. JMeter [11], which runs on a laptop, is used for the simulation of an appropriate user number (client) with parallel and identical invocations.

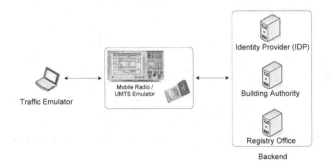

Fig. 7. Testbed for measurement of average response time

4.1 Test Setup and Results

The simulation process works as follows: It starts with one client, then 40, 80, 120 and finally 160, which perform parallel and identical invocations. Each step is repeated ten times (10 samples). Before using GMS, each authorized user has to be authenticated at the IDP in this scenario. GMS provides a fast search service for the request of a certain user activity of an appropriate user. The search parameters are then sent to all IGMS, which are installed on public authorities. The results are finally shown summarized to the user.

In order to determine the performance of authentication and authorization procedures within the IT-Federation / RB-SSO communication platform the response time parameter is measured by using the JMeter, which simulates the user number with concurrent same invocations. For UMTS a base station emulator [12] has been applied.

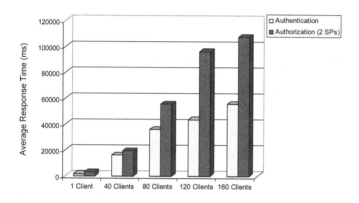

Fig. 8. Authentication at IDP and Authorization at two SPs

Figure 8 illustrates the average response time in terms of a certain number of simultaneous clients. The response time of both authorization processes at the SPs are summed up. It is shown that the time of an authorization process is much higher than the authentication for an increasing number of clients. The reason is the SAML communication procedure, which needs a lot of time for the authorization. Especially, the HTTP Redirect technology of SAML requires a high time need [13]. Furthermore, no redundant web servers are used for the scenario. It has to be noted that each user starts a new authorization, when a new sample/request is launched.

5 Visualization of Bottleneck Using Boolean Reliability Model

Using of analytical Boolean Reliability Model enables the detection of bottlenecks within a distributed IT-Federation [14]. In order to visualize the bottleneck, a reliability circuit has been designed from the RB-SSO communication platform (cf. fig. 9), which shows all relevant dependencies of the components within an IT-federation (IDP, SPs). Components are e.g. services of SAML, web server or tomcat.

Figure 9a shows that the components $x_{16}, x_{17}, x_{18}, x_{19}$ and x_{20} are an exemplary bottleneck, which represents a serial circuit. To increase the system availability, the serial circuit has to be replaced by a parallel circuit. The result from the optimization is depicted in Figure 9b where the x-axis displays the availability probability for each component. The y-axis presents the total system availability of the RB-SSO system.

The system availability function a_S (see fig. 9b) without redundancy is given by

$$a_S = S(a) = a^7 \cdot \left(1 - \left(1 - \left(1 - \left(1 - a^5\right)^3\right)\right)^2\right) \cdot \left(1 - (1-a)^{11}\right). \tag{1}$$

The system availability function a_S (see fig.9b) with redundancy is shown by

$$a_S = S(a) = a \cdot \left(1 - \left(1 - a^6\right)^2\right) \cdot \left(1 - \left(1 - \left(1 - \left(1 - a^5\right)^3\right)\right)^2\right) \cdot \left(1 - (1-a)^{11}\right). \tag{2}$$

It is obvious that the system with redundancy obtains better system availability. For the availability of 90% (a=0.9) for each component, the system with redundancy is up to 20 % better (see fig. 9b).

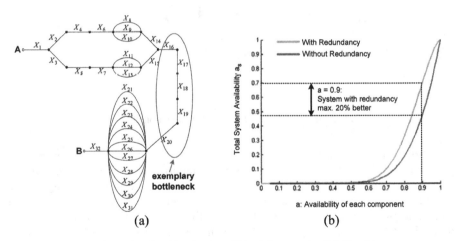

(a)   (b)

Fig. 9. Reliability Circuit (a) and Total System Availability (b)

6 Conclusion and Future Work

The MobisPro project develops and validates new concepts for a communication infrastructure in order to enable the mobile interoperability of distributed public authorities. The goal is the process optimization for preventive fire protection and reactive fire prevention. In this paper, we have presented the technical challenges and an approach for the development of such a communication platform. Furthermore, an exemplary Monitoring service is introduced to show, how distributed information systems can connect and communicate with each other in a secure manner.

The performance analysis has shown that using SAML requires an improvement of the communication procedures in order to obtain a better scalability. Particularly, the preventive fire protection needs a fast and efficient access to the distributed information. With the upcoming steps other reliability models (e.g. Markov Chains) have to be analyzed and developed to validate the reliability of the communication platform. In parallel, the development of a fast vertical handover algorithm and useful prioritization concept are the challenges for the future.

Acknowledgments. Our work has been conducted within the MobisPro-project, which is part of the SimoBIT program and funded by the German Ministry of Economics and Technology.

References

1. German Research Project MobisPro, http://www.mobis-pro.de
2. Wietfeld, C., Wolff, A.: MobileEmerGIS: a wireless-enabled technology platform to efficiently support field forces in protecting critical infrastructure. In: 2007 IEEE Conference on Technologies for Homeland Security, Woburn, USA (May 2007)
3. Goldack, M.: Lesson learned: From MS Passport to Cardspace, Stephen McGibbon's Web Journal, Horst Görtz Institute for IT-Security, Ruhr University Bochum (July 2006)
4. Liberty Alliance Project, http://www.projectliberty.org
5. Internet2, Shibboleth, http://shibboleth.internet2.edu/
6. Zhang, X., Li, Q., Qing, S., Zhang, H., Zhang, L.: A decentralized RBAC model and its user role administration. In: International Symposium on Communications and Information Technologies, 2007. ISCIT apos;2007, October 17-19, pp. 1280–1285 (2007)
7. OASIS Committee Draft, Technical Overview of OASIS Security Assertion Markup Language (SAML) V1.1 (2004)
8. IETF, The Transport Layer Security (TLS) Protocol Version 1.2, http://www.ietf.org
9. Zarrar Yousaf, F., Müller, C., Wietfeld, C.: Multi-Hop Discovery of Candidate Access Routers (MHD-CAR) for Fast Moving Mobile Nodes. In: 19th IEEE International Symposium on Personal, Indoor and Mobile Radio Communication (PIMRC), Cannes, France (September 2008)
10. Stewart, R.: Stream Control Transmission Protocol (2007), http://tools.ietf.org/html/rfc4960
11. J. A. Project, Apache JMeter, Jakarta Apache Project Homepage (2007), http://jakarta.apache.org/jmeter
12. Agilent Technologies, http://www.agilent.com
13. Takeda, Y., Kondo, S., Kitayama, Y., Torato, M., Motegi, T.: Avoidance of performance bottlenecks caused by HTTP redirect. identity management protocols. In: Conference on Computer and Communications Security, Proceeding of the second ACM workshop on Digital identity management, Virgina, USA (2006)
14. Fratta, L., Montanari, U.: A Boolean algebra method for computing the terminal reliability in a communication network. IEEE Transactions on Circuits Theory 20(3), 203–211 (1973)

Anonymity and Application Privacy in Context of Mobile Computing in eHealth

Daniel Slamanig, Christian Stingl, Christian Menard,
Martina Heiligenbrunner, and Jürgen Thierry

School of Medical Information Technology
Carinthia University of Applied Sciences
Primoschgasse 10, 9020 Klagenfurt, Austria
{slamanig,stingl,menard,heiligenbrunner,thierry}@cuas.at

Abstract. In the area of health care and sports in recent years a variety of mobile applications have been established. Mobile devices are of emerging interest due to their high availability and increasing computing power in many different health scenarios. In this paper we present a scalable secure sensor monitoring platform (SSMP) which collects vital data of users. Vital parameters can be collected by just one single sensor or in a multi-sensor configuration. Nowadays a wide spectrum of sensors is available which provide wireless connectivity (e.g. Bluetooth). Vital data can then easily be transmitted to a mobile device which subsequently transmits these data to an eHealth portal. There are already solutions implementing these capabilities, however privacy aspects of users are very often neglected. Since health data may enable people to draw potentially compromising conclusions (e.g. insurance companies), it is absolutely necessary to design an enhanced security concept in this context. To complicate matters further, the trustworthiness of providers which are operating with user's health data can not be determined by users a priori. This means that the security concept implemented by the provider may bear security flaws. Additionally there is no guarantee that the provider preserves the users privacy claims. In this work we propose a security concept incorporating privacy aspects using mobile devices for transferring and storing health data at a portal. In addition, the concept guarantees anonymity in the transfer process as well as for stored data at a service provider. Hence, insider attacks based on stored data can be prevented.

1 Introduction

Mobile devices like PDAs, smart phones or intelligent watches are of emerging interest in many different scenarios, due to their high availability and increasing computing power. In recent years, besides the telecommunication sector, a variety of applications have been established in the area of health care and sports. The main aspects in these fields are the acquisition and processing of vital parameters of users or sportsmen by mobile devices. An option is also the transmission of these data to subsequent information systems, which deal

J. Löffler and M. Klann (Eds.): Mobile Response, LNCS 5424, pp. 148–157, 2009.

with health related data. These systems are denoted as eHealth portals in this work. The transmission of data to eHealth portals is a crucial issue, since applications with decision support capabilities can analyze these data and make valuable decisions. By virtue of their sensitive character, health related data of users need to be protected against unauthorized access and manipulation. For instance, in Austria this is also written down in a national law. This law regulates measures which need to be considered when dealing with health related data. As a consequence, it is absolutely necessary in this context to design an appropriate security concept. To complicate matters further, the trustworthiness of providers which operate eHealth portals can not be determined by users a priori. This means that the security concept implemented by the provider may bear security flaws. Additionally the user has no guarantee that the provider always behaves as she would expect, i.e. to preserve the users privacy claims. The latter issue is reasonable since an actual study shows that more than 50% of all attacks against information systems are conducted by insiders [8]. This fact implies that the design of a trustable security concept can not solely be realized by the provider of an eHealth portal. In addition, the user's mobile device needs to be integrated in order to prevent insider threats. In particular, the mobile device should realize all privacy critical security aspects, e.g. encryption, decrytpion, key generation. Subsequently we present methods to design a security concept for mobile applications that is provably secure under standard cryptographic assumptions.

2 Privacy Enhancing Building Blocks

In this section we discuss the property anonymity with respect to a security concept for mobile applications. Furthermore we show how anonymity techniques can be used to enhance security concepts, especially concerning the privacy of users, with reasonable impact on the performance of the overall system.

Anonymity is often referred to as the property of being not identifiable with respect to a set of actions inside a group of people, the so called anonymity set $\mathcal{A}$ [12]. Intuitively the degree of anonymity is the higher, the larger $\mathcal{A}$ is and the more uniformly the actions are distributed within this set. We will subsequently consider anonymity in more detail, by defining different levels.

1. **Anonymous communication:** Anonymous communication is guaranteed, if an observer is not able to determine a communication relationship between two communicating parties.
2. **Sender- and receiver-anonymity:** A communication relationship between a sender and receiver provides sender-anonymity, if the receiver is not able to identify the sender by means of received messages. The receiver-anonymity can be defined analogously.
3. **Data anonymity:** A system provides data anonymity at the receiver, if data stored in the system and related to a specific sender can not be linked to the sender by the receiver and any other person. This means, that an

administrator of an eHealth portal is not able to establish a relationship between a patient and her related data. Consequently measures to provide data anonymity must be realized by the sender.

To further clarify these terms we will subsequently discuss two scenarios. In the first one we are considering an information portal, that offers medical information for the public. Since a person and her requested data (e.g. cancer, mental illness) are linkable, it is possible to draw potentially compromising conclusion about her. As a consequence and since the Internet does not offer anonymity on its own, it is recommendable to apply techniques that guarantee anonymous communication to prevent these statements. In this scenario sender- and receiver-anonymity and data anonymity are not necessary since the persons are solely requesting data without any identification at the service.

The second example considers a public eHealth portal, where registered users are able to manage their health related data. It must be mentioned that in general providers are not fully trustworthy. For instance, the security architecture at the eHealth portal and employees at the provider[1] represent uncertainty factors. If all anonymity properties mentioned above are realized, a person who uses this portal does not need to rely on trusting the provider anymore (e.g. concerning the divulgement of her data). Furthermore, additional security weaknesses at the provider, that may lead to unauthorized data access, do not influence the degree of privacy of person related data. In the following the three levels of anonymity will be discussed in detail.

2.1 Anonymous Communication

Especially when using the Internet, users often mistakenly believe in being anonymous. Even though $\mathcal{A}$ is large, this does not automatically imply a high level of anonymity. Open communication networks like the Internet, unfortuanetly do not implicitly provide mechanisms to guarantee anonymity. It is easy to eavesdrop the communication channel, apply traffic analysis and identify communicating parties, e.g. by means of their addresses (e.g. IP-address). While there exist widely deployed protocols like SSL/TLS or IPSec, which can be used to lock out eavesdroppers by means of cryptographic techniques, the anonymity aspect is often considered poorly. If anonymous communication systems are used, then the communication channel itself does not compromise the identities of communicating parties and can further be described by the properties unlinkability and unobservability. Whereas the first property means, that in a given system actions (e.g messages, the usage of services) can not be linked by an observer. The second one can be distinguished into sender-, receiver- and relationship-unobservability and can be described as the indistinguishability of subjects, performing actions within the system, from other non-active subjects within the set $\mathcal{A}$. Primitives to build anonymous communication systems were introduced by *Chaum* [6,7] and a lot of methods have been developed since that ([9,13,14] etc., see [10] for a sound overview). See also [1,2,20] for anonymous communication in context of

---

[1] It is not unusual, that employees are corrupt and divulge sensitive data.

mobile computing. We use anonymous channels to guarantee that independent server requests from a user cannot be linked via identifying information (e.g. IP-addresses) by an insider or an observer.

2.2   Sender- and Receiver-Anonymity

If we assume that we have a communication channel that guarantees perfect anonymity and unlinkability, then a user is connected to a service provider (server) via a kind of "magic channel" that leaks no information on the identity of the user. The main idea behind anonymous authentication is, that a user proves to the server the membership in a subset $\mathcal{U}' \subseteq \mathcal{U}$ (anonymity set) of authorized users $\mathcal{U}$, but the server does not gain any information on the identity of the user. Anonymous authentication was explicitly treated in [4,16] and can additionally be derived from group signatures (cf. [3]) and ring signatures [15]. As mentioned above, anonymous authentication does provide a mechanism that prevents the server from learning the user's identity. However, if a user wants to accomplish a set of transactions with the server, one of our main goals is to achieve that the server is not able to link these transactions. Obviously it would be possible to execute one anonymous authentication protocol for every single transaction. If these protocols include computation and communication intensive tasks (e.g. the use of general zero-knowledge protocols), this may turn out to be very time consuming. Thus an alternative approach is to use anonymous authentication protocols in conjunction with anonymous, unlinkable but authorized transactions based on tickets. The use of tickets or credentials is well known from pseudonym systems or anonymous credential systems (cf. [5]). However, if the credential issuer and verifier are the same entity, similar approaches to [19] can be used. We have designed a combination of both approaches, which can be described as follows. A user anonymously authenticates to the system and all subsequent transactions within a given time frame are accomplished on a ticket basis, which guarantees anonymity, unlinkability and yet authorization.

2.3   Data Anonymity

Recently we introduced a concept for data anonymity which is applicable for the use in eHealth portals [17,18]. This concept enables people to store and access data in a structured way using the infrastructure of a (potentially untrusted) service provider, so that solely qualified persons (the "owners" of data and people who were explicitly granted access rights) are able to determine which subset of data belong to them and are able to access them. A system based on this concept guarantees provable security based on standard cryptographic assumptions. One main objective for the design of the concept was a minimal impact on the efficiency of the system. In particular, using hierarchical data models this approach results in a constant number of additional cryptographic operations for each relationship between two object types.

3   Secure Sensor Monitoring Platform

The architecture of the secure sensor monitoring platform (SSMP) is organized
in three layers (see Figure 1), namely

- Acquisition Layer: This layer is responsible for the acquisition of sensor data
  and the transfer of these data to the eHealth portal.
- Application Layer: The application layer represents the eHealth portal which
  is responsible for the storage of the data and provides web-based access.
- Security Layer: The security layer is responsible for a secure and anonymous
  communication between the acquisition layer and the application layer.

Subsequently we will briefly discuss the acquisition and the application layer
and in detail the security layer. This is due to the fact, that this paper focuses
primarily on security and anonymity aspects regarding the use of mobile devices
in context of an eHealth portal.

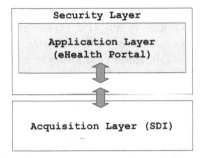

Fig. 1. Three layers of the SSMP architecture

3.1   Acquisition Layer

The data acquisition is based on a so-called sensor data infrastructure (SDI)
which is currently implemented as a prototype. At the moment we have integrated an ECG and a pulse sensor. In the future it should be possible to integrate
various sensors using a standardized interface. The sensors are connected to the
mobile device either via a simple serial interface using cables or a wireless solution like Bluetooth, WLAN-connectivity or a similar technology. The minimum
configuration consists of a single sensor (e.g. temperature) connected to a mobile
device using Bluetooth technology and GPRS to transfer the collected data to
the eHealth portal. Because of the scalability of this approach, the system can
easily be extended to a multi-sensor infrastructure for instance integrated into
a smart home environment.

3.2   Application Layer

The two main issues of the application layer are firstly the management of stored
sensor data and corresponding metadata and secondly the visualization and

analysis of the sensor data. In our prototype we focused on the former aspect which is most relevant for the proof of concept of the security architecture. Another main topic will be the design of a web-based user interface to enable users to manage and analyze their data as well as to possibly make decisions.

3.3 Security Layer

In this application we have established a public-key infrastructure (PKI) which provides public key certificates to every single user. Any user who participates in the system has to possess a private key and the certificate containing the corresponding public key. The PKI is based on X.509 v3 certificates and the RSA cryptosystem for en-/decryption and digital signatures is used.

Anonymous Communication: Since mobile devices are connected to limitations regarding the computational resources and methods for anonymous communication require time consuming operations in the bootstrapping (route setup) as well as in the communication phase, a proxy-based approach is applied (see Figure 2). The proxy-server (anonymity provider) operates a VPN-gateway which is used by the mobile device to initially establish a VPN tunnel to provide data confidentiality and data integrity. The anonymity provider furthermore operates a Java Anon Proxy (JAP)[2] which is solely able to forward anonymous HTTP-requests of the mobile device and an additional TOR-client[3]. The latter one is able to forward any TCP-based service request. Any anonymous request is established through the VPN tunnel via the anonymity provider.

Anonymous Authentication: For anonymous authentication a modified protocol which was proposed in [11,16] is realized. The subset (anonymity set) used for anonymous authentication in our application must contain at least $k = 100$ users. Hence, the probability to identify a specific authenticating user in an anonymity set is less or equal $1/100$. The above mentioned protocol requires the authenticator to evaluate $k - 1$ public-key encrypted values in order to reveal a potentially cheating verifier. In our context and due to the limited computational resources of mobile devices, we propose to reduce these evaluations to m, $k - 1 \ll m \geq 10$. Hence, the probability to reveal a cheating verifier will be reduced to $p = 1 - 2^{-m}$ which is reasonable for practical purposes. Within this anonymous authentication an initially blinded ticket T_i (cf. [19]) is created by the client and digitally signed by the verifier. The authenticator obtains the signed ticket $\bar{T}_i$ by unblinding T_i, whereas T_i and $\bar{T}_i$ are unlinkable.

Anonymous Unlinkable and Authorized Transactions: The above mentioned unblinded ticket $\bar{T}_i$ is used to anonymously authorize the subsequent transaction within the system. During this transaction a new blinded ticket T_{i+1} is again digitally signed by the verifier. In order to avoid misuse of tickets, they are solely valid in a predefined period of time. Additionally, every ticket can only be used for one transaction, since the system checks for "double-spending".

---

[2] http://anon.inf.tu-dresden.de
[3] http://www.torproject.org

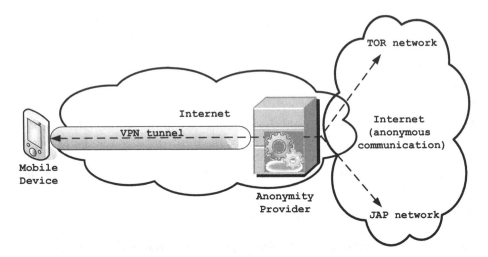

Fig. 2. A mobile device creates a VPN tunnel to a gateway (anonymity provider) and chooses the appropriate anonymity service (JAP, TOR) which is provided by the anonymity provider

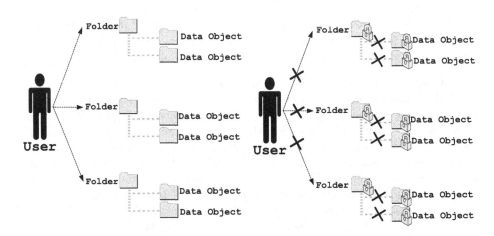

Fig. 3. This picture illustrates a schematic model of an eHealth portal which consists of users, folders and data objects. By applying methods for data anonymity the data objects are encrypted, authorization is realized by means of shares and all relationships between subjects and objects are "hidden" by means of pseudonymization.

Data Anonymity: In this application data anonymity is realized by means of the following aspects

- Confidentiality: Every data object of the system is stored symmetrically encrypted using a symmetric key k, whereas all cryptographic operations are performed by the mobile device.

- Authorization: The symmetric key k which is unique for every data object is encrypted for every authorized user with her public key (share). The user whose data are stored in the system is obviously the first authorized user. Every authorized user is consequently able to grant access to further users.
- Pseudonymization: Additionally to the above mentioned methods all relationships between subjects and objects in the system (e.g. users, folders, and data objects) are pseudonymized [17,18]. This is realized by means of user-generated encrypted pseudonyms. Hence, only persons which are in possession of the corresponding cryptographic key are able to reveal the pseudonym and consequently the related objects. It must be mentioned, that this relation can not be determined without the knowledge of the corresponding cryptographic key.

Thus, an insider is not able to gain any information on stored data and their relationships without explicit authorization.

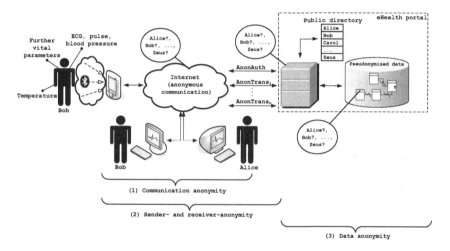

Fig. 4. Schematic overview of the Secure Sensor Monitoring Platform (SSMP). User Bob anonymously authenticates (AnonAuth) to the eHealth portal using an anonymous communication channel. He transmits his data (AnonTrans) anonymously to the eHealth portal, whereas the data is stored in a pseudonymized fashion. Later on Bob is able to access his data anonymously via his home PC or may even share his data with Alice.

4   Conclusion

A study performed in 2007 [8] shows, that more than 50% of attacks on a system are conducted by insiders. As a consequence it is crucial that insider attacks are carefully taken into consideration when designing security concepts. This is fundamental if applications deal with person realted data and especially with health related data, which are classified as sensitive data. In this paper we have discussed and introduced methods that provide anonymity on different levels in the context of mobile applications. These techniques can be used to improve the user's privacy and consequently enhance the user's trust in such applications. In our opinion this is a fundamental aspect when dealing with sensitive data and mobile applications and can contribute to a more common use of these applications.

References

1. Andersson, C., Lundin, R., Fischer-Hübner, S.: Privacy Enhanced WAP Browsing with mCrowds – Anonymity Properties and Performance Evaluation of the mCrowds System. In: Proceedings of the ISSA 2004 Enabling Tomorrow Conference, Gallagher Estate, Midrand, South Africa, June 30-July 2 (2004)
2. Andersson, C., Panchenko, A.: Practical Anonymous Communication on the Mobile Internet using Tor. In: Proceedings of the Third International Workshop on the Value of Security through Collaboration (IEEE SECOVAL 2007) part of IEEE SECURECOMM 2007, Nice, France (September 2007)
3. Ateniese, G., Camenisch, J., Joye, M., Tsudik, G.: A Practical and Provably Secure Coalition-Resistant Group Signature Scheme. In: Bellare, M. (ed.) CRYPTO 2000. LNCS, vol. 1880, pp. 255–270. Springer, Heidelberg (2000)
4. Boneh, D., Franklin, M.: Anonymous Authentication with Subset Queries. In: Proc. of ACM Conference on Computer and Communications Security, pp. 113–119 (1999)
5. Camenisch, J., Lysyanskaya, A.: An Efficient System for Non-transferable Anonymous Credentials with Optional Anonymity Revocation. In: Pfitzmann, B. (ed.) EUROCRYPT 2001. LNCS, vol. 2045, pp. 93–118. Springer, Heidelberg (2001)
6. Chaum, D.: Untraceable electronic mail, return addresses, and digital pseudonyms. Commun. ACM 24(2), 84–90 (1981)
7. Chaum, D.: Security without identification: transaction systems to make big brother obsolete. Commun. ACM 28(10), 1030–1044 (1985)
8. Computer Crime and Security Survey 2007, Computer Security Institute, http://www.gocsi.com/forms/csi_survey.jhtml
9. Dingledine, R., Mathewson, N., Syverson, P.: Tor: The Second-Generation Onion Router. In: Proc. of the 13th USENIX Security Symposium (August 2004)
10. Danezis, G., Diaz, C.: A survey of anonymous communication channels. Technical Report MSR-TR-2008-35, Microsoft Research (January 2008)
11. Lindell, A.: Anonymous Authenticaion. Whitepaper Aladdin Knowledge Systems (2007), http://www.aladdin.com/blog/pdf/AnonymousAuthentication.pdf
12. Pfitzmann, A., Köhntopp, M.: Anonymity, Unobservability, and Pseudonymity – A Proposal for Terminology. In: Federrath, H. (ed.) Designing Privacy Enhancing Technologies. LNCS, vol. 2009, pp. 1–9. Springer, Heidelberg (2001)
13. Pfitzmann, A., Pfitzmann, B., Waidner, M.: ISDN- Mixes: Untraceable Communication with Very Small Bandwidth Overhead. In: Proc. Kommunikation in verteilten Systemen (KiVS). IFB 267, pp. 451–463. Springer, Berlin (1991)
14. Reiter, M.K., Rubin, A.D.: Crowds: Anonymity for Web Transactions. Technical Report 97-15, Center for Discrete Mathematics & Theoretical Computer Science (1997)
15. Rivest, R., Shamir, A., Tauman, Y.: How to leak a secret. In: Boyd, C. (ed.) ASIACRYPT 2001. LNCS, vol. 2248, pp. 552–565. Springer, Heidelberg (2001)

16. Schechter, S., Parnell, T., Hartemink, A.: Anonymous Authentication of Membership in Dynamic Groups. In: Franklin, M.K. (ed.) FC 1999. LNCS, vol. 1648, pp. 184–195. Springer, Heidelberg (1999)
17. Slamanig, D., Stingl, C., Lackner, G., Payer, U.: Privacy Protection in web-based Multiuser-Systems (German). In: Horster, P. (ed.) DACH-Security 2007, pp. 98–110. IT-Verlag (2007)
18. Slamanig, D., Stingl, C.: Privacy Aspects of eHealth. In: Proceedings of the Third International Conference on Availability, Reliability and Security (ARES 2008), pp. 1226–1233. IEEE Computer Society Press, Los Alamitos (2008)
19. Syverson, P.F., Stubblebine, S.G., Goldschlag, D.M.: Unlinkable Serial Transactions. In: Luby, M., Rolim, J.D.P., Serna, M. (eds.) FC 1997. LNCS, vol. 1318, pp. 39–55. Springer, Heidelberg (1997)
20. Tatli, E.I., Stegemann, D., Lucks, S.: Dynamic Mobile Anonymity with Mixing. Technical Report TR-2006-007, Department for Mathematics and Computer Science, University of Mannheim, March 27 (2006)

Author Index